THE CONTROL OF THE SOCIAL MIND

THE CONTROL OF THE SOCIAL MIND

PSYCHOLOGY OF ECONOMIC AND POLITICAL RELATIONS

by

ARLAND D. WEEKS

DEAN OF THE SCHOOL OF EDUCATION OF THE NORTH DAKOTA AGRICULTURAL COLLEGE, FARGO; AUTHOR OF "THE EDUCATION OF TO-MORROW;" THE PSYCHOLOGY OF CITIZENSHIP," "SOCIAL ANTAGONISMS," ETC.

GYAN

Published by

GYAN

Gyan Publishing House
5, Ansari Road
Daryaganj, New Delhi-110002
Phone: 011-47034999, 9811692060
E-mail: books@gyanbooks.com

Distribution Network
gyanbooks.com
India, USA, Canada, UK, Australia, France

ISBN : 978-81-212-2305-8 (PB)
First Published, 1923

2nd Impression 2021

Printed at: Gyan Press, Delhi.

The Control of the Social Mind
Author: Arland D. Weeks

THE CONTROL OF THE SOCIAL MIND

PSYCHOLOGY OF ECONOMIC AND POLITICAL RELATIONS

BY

ARLAND D. WEEKS

DEAN OF THE SCHOOL OF EDUCATION OF THE NORTH DAKOTA AGRICULTURAL COLLEGE, FARGO; AUTHOR OF "THE EDUCATION OF TO-MORROW," "THE PSYCHOLOGY OF CITIZENSHIP," "SOCIAL ANTAGONISMS," ETC.

D. APPLETON AND COMPANY
NEW YORK :: 1923 :: LONDON

INTRODUCTION

The present volume considers the resources and operations, and the direction of the more public phases of mental behavior. It sets forth the basis of social conduct: what nature supplies for the complex life demanded of the citizen of to-day, and what human effort has done and must continue to do to bring the processes of socialization to a reasonable efficiency. Social psychology has come to occupy the centre of the stage; and much that is written and spoken in its name shows more familiarity with the terminology than with vital activities and their inner nature. Professor Weeks' treatment is intimate and realistic, almost clinical in the sense that it imparts of social bonds and relations experienced in actual contacts, not formulated in arm-chair principles. Yet it is the special function of the man of science—the psychologist in this instance—to make articulate the knowledge and the wisdom born of the practical life, and give it a local habitation as well as a name in the mental possessions of the responsible reflective man. "In psychology as in other fields of science there is an advantage in bringing familiar things into vividness by expert analysis and clearer definition." This programme is as skillfully executed as it is well conceived.

The programme involves the selective survey of human psychology that provides the available material for the operation of social forces. These in turn fall into two groups: the more general factors of the psychic make-up, the deeper and older sources of conduct and motive; and the special and more refined operations of the mental mechanisms employed in adaptation to the modern life. The latter are reserved for a "close-up" projection. There is enforced the lesson that "primitive mind underlies the most cultivated mind of to-day"; that older trends may be diverted and controlled but not wholly displaced; that the human mind was formed early with no "late change in fundamental mentality" to meet the needs of modern civilization. We must continue to build all progress upon the available raw material of our original nature. A further clue lies in the psychology of childhood. We are born in a modern world and receive the set of our expressions in an intensely busy, highly complicated, modern environment, artificial to the last degree and the latest fashion; we have no primitive experience and slight fitness to sense its nature. But we can find a working pattern of some of its drives and motives, its urges and handicaps, its trials and triumphs, in the critical interpretation of child-behavior and our own adult reconstruction of its experiences. We have all grown up—some successfully and the majority imperfectly—and through that evolution obtain a vivid impression of the meaning alike of disposition and of adjustment. Tapping this evolutionary stream at whatever point, we come upon suggestive illustrations of its source and flow. A consideration of habit, defense, and resistance will answer to tell the tale and point the moral.

The childish insistence that things once thus done must continue in the same ritual or arouse emotional upset, the rigid conservatism of primitive custom and taboo, and the needless friction of precedent or the reactionary adherence to the status quo, are psychologically of a nature all compact. The service of this conservative trend is indispensable and yet illustrates how "one good custom can corrupt the world." By way of moral, the virtue of mobility is emphasized. "The most efficient type of person for social change is one who has a large and stable body of useful fundamental habits and who is comparatively free from habit, or is habitually elastic where new responses are indicated." Habit, however, is but a summary name for conduct whose true nature appears only when referred to the guiding mechanism, including the motive. Instinct summarizes the primary stage, so characteristically adequate for certain ranges of animal behavior and so loosely organized in man: "Man lacks precise mental specialization at birth." The modification and supplementation of instinct under the tuition of analyzed experience makes habit; and this in turn yields to the maturer direction of reason,—the supreme human endowment and privilege. From the direction of behavior by reason—in the individual and the social application—have arisen the processes and benefits of civilization. But all this in no simple fashion: the contest is not grossly between instinct and habit, or between habit and reason but between tangled motives of all origins,—more particularly and commonly, "rational and less rational mind are set against each other at many points." "The strike is a notable example of an instinctive rather than a rational attempt to correct evils."

The mechanisms of defense are suggestive for the social application of deep-seated tendencies. In the lower ranges the equipment is physical, by tooth and claw and horn and fang, rather than by wit. Among the psychical defenses are mentioned the falsehood-defense; the back-seat defense; and the evasion defense,—all temptations for human frailty, and parents of social sin. To lie, to pretend, to assume, to bluff, to deceive, seem as natural outlets of expression in the commercial world of to-day as in cruder times and more direct situations. Strategy, diplomacy, propaganda—which is "twin brother to advertising"—are all accredited as well as easily discredited enterprises. Withdrawal, and the train of social fears which it implies, is similarly the parent of the prudential virtues and of the cowardly and obsessional vices. Evasion—by reason of the Freudian emphasis—has assumed a conspicuous place in psychology. It represents the route of escape to an imaginary world, more comfortably moulded to desire than the rough and imperfect habitation of reality. Natural and desirable as a refuge for the child, the world of the imagination may become a menace for the primitive man who peoples it with hostile dreads and obsessions, and may become an enervating, disqualifying trend in the complex social situation of to-day. "Whatever mires mind in illusion and upholsters it in the fanciful is directly opposed to the making of a better real world." Yet the seer of visions has a foremost place in progress, and without the idealist the people perish.

The boundary between individual and social psychology—like every enclosure, at once a bond and a barrier—is brought to expression in suggestion and authority, both as techniques of the control of conduct alike of the individual and of the social mind, and in their foundations in original traits. The child is fortunately suggestible, and not quite so fortunately is the primitive man and the mildly sophisticated citizen,—his nearest representative in the modern democratic milieu. The child, the savage, the citizen must all yield to authority; without it there is chaos and disrule. The temptation of authority to impose is the besetting sin of tyranny and the lure of power, as less seriously are the patronising superiority complex and the parental dominance and economic abuses of capital and labor alike. On the one side the tendency to submit, to follow, to look for, accept, and even crave direction; on the other hand to command, to lead, to assert, to dominate, to impose one's will.

The fact that the social will thus expressed assumes many forms, from arbitrary autocracy to constituted force democratically organized and reasonably administered, brings about the situation that the opponents in the tendency to lead and the tendency to follow are arrayed as in a contest between the individual and the group. The individual bows to the social will while yet he protests; his protest is in the interests of individuality and self-respect; he seeks a difficult loyalty at once to his own opinions and to the social consensus. It is in this narrow channel that the ship of personal career as well as the ship of state often find difficult sailing, with many tacks to the winds of compromise. Primitive servility will not answer. The modern citizen must learn to be critical as well as assertive; his social value implies a solution of the tendency to lead and the tendency to follow, each adjusted to the other, to retain the indispensable morale of initiative on the one hand and of coöperation on the other. He must resist unwise propaganda, specious argument, plausible suggestion, as well as unjust authority; yet retain wide sympathies and the open public-mindedness that furnishes the basis of progressive citizenship.

While these illustrations are typical of the temper in which the psychology underlying social behavior is set forth, every phase of the intricate mosaic of human nature is so distinctive in its pattern that it is only in the cumulative result that the design appears. The play motives and play expressions have a notable part in making man the particular kind of social animal that he is. Closely allied is the constructive motive; and both in turn hark back to the need of variety and the stimulation of change. How to satisfy the need of play, of creative desire, and of variety, under the stress of livelihood and the competitions of modern demands is no easy matter; yet all the higher public interests wait upon the fair satisfaction of personal needs. Since so much energy must be spent in wage-earning occupations, it becomes a supremely important problem to inject into such work the largest measure of psychological compensations,—at the minimum to avoid the distressing issues of their total disregard. Deadening routine, apathy from absence of interest, despondency from loss of hope or ambition, unrest from a sense of injustice, are all formidable handicaps to the efficient personal life of adjusted content, and exercise a commanding influence upon economic and political movements which register these imponderables of peace, so readily converted into the realities of social war.

There are moreover certain peculiar and higher-grade requirements that may properly be expected of the high-grade citizen. Among these Professor Weeks selects for apt consideration the proper use of memory in interpreting the lessons of history, and the desirability of accuracy in perception in finding one's way responsibly among the clamoring appeals of self-interest and showy propaganda.

The chapter on the "Art of Accuracy" may be commended as an apt lesson in psychology, and as an illustration of the selection of the happy phrase and the illuminating analysis which pervades the entire work, and is the result not of a verbal facility but of a capacity for clearing the decks to fighting trim before venturing upon the enterprise of exposition.

Professor Weeks' major purpose is centered upon the civic consciousness and the civic conscience, which must be shaped from the materials of human nature, and upon which directly depends the actual operation of public concerns. As is true of every application, there comes a point at which the special knowledge of the applier supersedes in immediate value the more theoretical insight of the philosopher and guide. The principles of the psychology of advertising or of the political mind must give way to the concrete details of the technic of advertisement and the machinery of politics. Yet the psychologist's occupation is not gone, when he takes the second place. He can still trace in this pragmatic field the operation of personal initiative and self-interest as against the "sprawling anonymity" of public service, and indicate why common welfare lags behind private interests, can make clearer why coöperation is difficult to achieve, and why what is everybody's business is apt to become nobody's business. He can set forth the direction or further changes in human nature which must be made effective before the campaign against war can be converted from an idealistic enterprise to a practical policy, can outline "what escape there is from the raw force and pattern of jealousy, envy, rivalry, disparagement, competition, dispraise," and all the narrower motivations that stand in the way of social progress. He can make it plain what qualities should be fostered, what technics of honor and social approval should be instituted to bring about the selection of the best citizens for the highest service. He can conclude optimistically or otherwise that "the future belongs to the great natural motivations of instinct illuminated by logical analysis, developed attention, self-restraint, verified knowledge, and disciplined imagination." Man will never rise above the level of his inherent qualities. As through these he has achieved a notable triumph in the control of physical nature and thus transformed the face of the earth and the appearance of his environment, so it remains to achieve a comparable revolution in his social milieu by the control of the social mind. The unemployed resources for this consummation are many and vast; to realize them will require the most skillful employment of the principles of social psychology harnessed to the machinery of practical progress.

Professor Weeks has established his position as a director of ideas for popular consumption by his former works upon "The Psychology of Citizenship," "The Education of To-morrow," "Social Antagonisms," etc.

He combines in unusual manner the art of the expositor with the appreciation of the attitude and needs of the student. In the present volume he finds a theme congenial to his methods and close to his educational interests. His purpose is that of the series, of which this volume forms a welcome addition, to convey in simple language, yet with the background and authority of well established principles, the lessons and the spirit of selected phases of modern psychology.

JOSEPH JASTROW

CONTENTS

PART I

FUNDAMENTALS AND THEIR APPLICATIONS

I

CONTROL THROUGH PSYCHOLOGY

An increasing use of psychology is being made for effecting desirable adjustments. No longer is the worker regarded as merely a mechanical unit of production, nor the first offender as an incurable instance of depravity. In industry and penology the psychological viewpoint dictates new procedures. The economist, the judge and the lawyer, through giving greater heed to mental phenomena, tend to pursue different courses than formerly. In education both discipline and instruction have been revolutionized by specific effort to understand the child. The advertiser has become an adept in commercial control through utilizing laws of habit and suggestion. Through analysis of motives the modern student of history finds fresh clues to the explanation of early events and becomes better able to interpret present trends and contemporary happenings. Such ancient practices as sacrifice and pilgrimage become intelligible under the fuller knowledge of instincts and motivation. The application of psychology in medicine is notable, whether within the medical profession or in related activities outside this profession.

More is known about the mind than formerly, and we are more given to employing concretely the available information. The point of attack on many problems has shifted from the physical to the mental. As physical science was the crowning contribution of the last century, so psychological method promises to be a signal achievement of the present. The forces with which men consciously and explicitly deal are increasingly the mental energies. Progress will be judged more in terms of mental reactions than in terms of physical creations like skyscrapers and steel ships. Society is undergoing a transformation by a shift of emphasis from body to brain. Trade and legislation, domestic relations and municipal government will be more definitely directed with reference to the ascertained facts and promise of human behavior.

The program of physical science was announced by Francis Bacon, its great visionary, to be the amelioration of the lot of man; so and even more certainly may be announced the prospect of psychology. Great as are the contributions of physical science, there is disappointment; the world is not yet what it should be. The menace of lethal gas is sufficient warning that the continuing welfare of the race must involve a technic of control through reflection, a utilization of the undeveloped resources and of the raw materials for happier forms of intelligence.

It is a well-known fact that knowledge of a principle does not guarantee its application. One may accept or preach one thing and rather innocently practice another. A person who knows that oil will float on water—knows it as a principle—may be the first to throw water on an oil fire. One must know that water thrown on an oil fire will spread the fire. This is an additional fact—a fact of application. Without the fact of application the knowledge of the principle, while interesting, is practically useless—momentarily useless. Similarly in the field of psychology. One may know the force of mental suggestion and yet not think of its application in important relations. To vitalize knowledge of psychology by extensive and ingenious application is an inviting educational ideal.

Of far-reaching importance are the applications of known laws of mental behavior to social and civic relations and problems. The gravest problems to-day are those of social and community affairs, and of national and international relations. In this field there is need of bringing the knowledge of psychology to bear on specific difficulties. The price of failure here is not such as we should contemplate with tranquil spirits, for civilization is at stake.

Higher social welfare must be achieved with such materials as general society affords. The "intelligence quotient" of the average man may remain little changed. Indeed, the raw materials are presumably fairly adequate if resourcefully employed. It was said by Elbert Hubbard that the man who could not build up a business with the help that he could employ was not the man to build up the business. Man does not naturally fly nor remain under water; but he does both successfully by artifice. Inventors did not despair because in many respects the physical equipment of man is poor and limited. The deficiencies have been overcome by contrivance. In like manner it is possible to supply by contrivance and supplement by system the deficiencies which all men show more or less for civic functions and social progress. We shall get nowhere by deploring the limitations of the prevailing native endowment of intelligence.

Control through psychology should be dissociated

from any suggestion of clever manipulation for selfish ends. Superior faculties have superior place in the very nature of things; but in the development of the technic of civic psychology there can properly be no more hint of sinister uses or exploitative purpose than can be admitted in the enlightened constitutionalism of liberal politics. Psychology can indicate the mechanisms and resources; a social-moral conscience must set the course to be followed.

II

THE SOCIAL MIND

In essence all human psychology is social, in that the mental behavior is socialized. Our powers and traits have come into being under family and group conditions. The social imprint is written all over man's mind. Instincts, emotions, motives, language—all have a social reference. With no one to look on, how long could a Robinson Crusoe keep alive the motive to excel or maintain an interest in his personal appearance? What would become of language without the presence of others with whom one could communicate? If language were not, how much thought would be possible, lacking its vehicle and preservative? Even righteous indignation implies the evildoer, present or absent. One may feel the emotion of anger when dealing with inanimate objects; but when such is the case he transfers a reaction originating in association with his fellow creatures.

The field of social psychology includes as a study

of processes, mental reactions in the manifold relationships of the individual to society; and as a study of products, the many outcomes of mind in social institutions, such as law, religion, fashion, custom, art, morals, and language. The formation of public opinion, the craze and fad, the public meeting and the mob demand consideration in every comprehensive treatment. The social relations of the individual form the story of his life—his relations to the family, and to economic, professional, political, cultural, and educational organizations, besides the various situations of informal contact. There are as many psychological situations as there are situations; the psychological moment constantly recurs. The present purpose is to consider aspects of mind that have special significance for further social development and better ways of getting on together.

What advantage has psychology as a science over plain knowledge of human nature? There is the advantage that any organized branch of knowledge has over knowledge of the casual type; a person can command more in a shorter time. From hit-and-miss observation and experience everybody knows something about physics and mechanics; but a systematic study goes far beyond haphazard experience. In a lifetime the average person would not acquire more than a small part of the knowledge of physics that he could obtain in months from physics formulated as a science.

Psychology impresses the method of science—observation, impartial interpretation, cautious generalization; above all it emphasizes that the phenomena of mind are part and parcel of the things that are amenable to study and scientific approach. For centuries man regarded himself as an exception to natural laws. This attitude through gradual change has been dispelled. Developments in psychology as well as in the social sciences indicate that the concept of cause and effect, of environment and product, has entered far into our reasoning upon social problems.

In psychology, as in other fields of science, there is an advantage in bringing familiar things into vividness by expert analysis and clearer definition. Grammar may be studied profitably if only to pass in review processes of speech that go on habitually. To face reflectively the elements of our habitual acts tends to establish a new viewpoint and encourages progress. It is worth while to view ourselves objectively in the mirror that psychology holds up to human nature.

Social change is furthered by modern psychology through its affiliations with evolutionary biology. Dynamic suggestiveness is no small asset to social welfare; much mischief has been due to the standstill frame of mind. Progress becomes the actual program of the world's affairs. Any group of men to-day, if asked whether they look for different and better conditions twenty-five years from now, would vote *yes*. The spirit outcropping from the evolutionary view permeates society. Civilization is likely to arrive sooner in its fullness through belief in development. Even the individual to-day seems less to regard himself as capable of reaching a stage beyond which improvement is impossible.

The common expectation of change and improvement in individual and society gives point to studies of mind and results in fuller knowledge. Man lived on the earth for thousands of years without knowing as much about its size, character and position as a ten-year-old schoolboy knows to-day. Similarly the earlier observations on the mental man were deficient. Marked advance has taken place in the understanding of human endowment and of its responses to environment; and no less in generalization, point of view, and command of data. The biological point of view applied to human traits has made as wide a change in the field of psychology as was made in cosmogony by the Copernican astronomy, or in medicine by the germ theory of disease. The treatment of the child, views regarding the criminal and the insane, industrial psychology, propaganda—these suggest how large the change.

Not only does the individual need to know as much as possible of psychology for his own survival and welfare, but society in its collective aspects can thrive only by recognition of mental forces. Knowledge of psychology is required for the wise management of public and national affairs. After the late prostration of the nations it is evident that public affairs have gone forward too little illuminated by studies of social mind, analogous to those studies that have advanced the world in its material aspects.

In public affairs the relative backwardness may be ascribed to the fact that social nature has been less systematically studied than has physical nature. The social mind has yet to be studied adequately for purposes of better and happier living. Social forces and phenomena are more complex and evasive than life cycles of insects, or the principles of levers, or the mechanics of liquids. While physical science has advanced notably, knowledge of the mind in social situations is still in its early stages. Much remains to be done by way of inventory of mental assets capable of utilization for the the career of civilization. A larger science of mind is possible with corresponding improvement of social relationships and administration.

Such a science contemplates a rational and constructive use of social forces. Resources of reflection are capable of more efficient and less injurious uses. In our physical civilization constructive use has oftentimes been made of unpromising materials. Flood waters have been impounded to irrigate orchards; animals and plants have been domesticated and made to serve the purposes of society; the severities of climate have been mitigated by intelligent adaptations of fuel and clothing; barriers of distance vanish with the locomotive and radio. In the psychology of human engineering there are presumably as great possibilities as have been demonstrated in the field of mechanics and physical science. An excessive amount of friction and discord appears in the social cosmos; human energy goes to waste or is diverted to the infliction of grave injury, as in mob action and war.

The better direction of the energies of consciousness presupposes point of view and data. The psychological attitude toward social problems becomes the starting point for pronounced departures in method. Even the time-honored notion that human nature never changes casts no blight upon the promise of rationalizing the social order, for it is possible with existing materials to build the social structure into a different architecture. The crux of the matter is how traits and tendencies of human nature are developed and employed. The same bricks build structures of widely contrasting effects. The best possible world will consist of people whose traits and tendencies are utilized in the best possible manner.

The variety of occasions for psychological procedure is wide indeed, for there is no reflective behavior in any field that does not present possibilities of superior method. From casual daily experience to the affairs of nations, psychologizing promises to eliminate friction and open paths of harmonious and constructive effort; the serious antagonisms of society may be resolved and finer coördinations achieved. Social disorder implies defects of method. The laws of mind, brought precisely to bear upon social difficulties, promise insight, and such insight wisely directed makes possible results comparable in perfection to those produced by the application of the laws of physics in the harmony of the artificial world of a laboratory.

III

RESPONSE OF MIND TO ENVIRONMENT

Early man, by reason of his anatomical structure, was unique in physical adaptability. He escaped the anatomical specialization which was a limiting factor in the case of lower animals. Consider what a strangely unadaptable creature is the horse or dog. The lower animals grew specialized for defense or flight or food. Man was less specialized, and adaptable; for him the door was open for progress and free life on the planet. The human hand is a wonderful anatomical tool. Man has multiplied his problems and added immeasurably to the thought-compelling character of physical environment by building huts and houses, taming wild beasts, and stirring the soil in agriculture. The lower animals in the course of the remote past became specialized in response to fixed units of environment and remained on low levels. Escaping fixedness of condition, through pioneering to new environments and ultimately creating a new world of novel appliances to react upon intelligence, man, the supreme physiological machine, became unique in cerebral resources.

Physical equipment of generalized type became supplemented by unique brain power; otherwise the limit of human development would early have been reached. Physical adaptability can go so far and no further. The body can make certain adjustments to climate; for example, the skin undergoes some change at the advent of cold weather, but the most economical and successful adaptation to cold is through the intelligence that borrows the skins of wild animals or weaves textiles or transports coal for fuel. Increasingly in the struggle to keep alive and comfortable, man has utilized intelligence; and invention has taken the place of physical modification. As an organ of adaptation the brain has demonstrated its superiority; man, replying on certain mental functionings, "bestrides the narrow earth like a colossus." He has exploited nature and fairly conquered the physical menaces and hazards that otherwise would have reduced his numbers and have made him a slave instead of a commanding force in his contact with nature.

The intelligence utilized in man's struggle with nature has been of comparatively primitive type.

Indeed the prehistoric mind is the substructure of contemporary mind.

We share in the inheritance of the prehistoric mind—the mind of the cave man and the raw-meat eater, the hairy man. Back in the eons when the prairie grasses were laying down the humus that is now soil below the surface of a wheat field, and when the waves had begun to chafe the pebble that is now sand, the pattern of the mind of the university graduate was being traced. It was then that fundamental interests, aversions, raging appetites, fears, sly trickery, bellowing melodrama and "big stick" technic were characteristic responses to environmental conditions. Early man haunted the beaches and river beds in search of food—who would eat an oyster except through atavism? The cave grandmother had to pick and pry at things out of protective curiosity—and her modern descendant surreptitously fingers linings in the cloakroom. The human instincts, general aptitudes and abilities and the characteristic behavior of attention, memory, association of ideas, reasoning and problem-solving became functions of human intelligence in the remote past. This is not to say, for example, that the fear tendency has not undergone modification or that we have to-day exactly the same coördination of faculties as prevailed at the time when the brain cavity first reached modern proportions, but that the native tendencies and capacities of the mind are referable to archaic origin, and that the primitive mind underlies the most cultivated mind of to-day.

The nature of the primitive environment can indeed be speculatively inferred from modern mind. In many ways the tendencies we see within—our fears, rages, suspicions, desire to hunt, kill and see horrible sights, our monogamy by determination, the soothing lapse to wilds of wood and water, the indecision between coöperation and murder—enable us through imagination to reconstruct the life of the sordid mire-camp and the soaked tree-dwelling with its one warm spot of attachment.

Certain it is that modern civilization has come without late change in fundamental mentality. The changes that may be wrought later in the character of civilization will need to be made with old mind, but old mind redirected. Hereditary human nature changes, of course, but slowly, even as the dog's nature is rather different from that of his wolf ancestor. But changes in fundamental mind are too slow in coming, particularly in the absence of eugenics, to be of much promise. The saving fact for social reconstruction is that, without disavowal of original tendencies, there lies within the power of education and social control the vast resource of redirecting the expression of human nature and substituting preferred activities for those condemned by experience.

As an instance of civilization by substitution, consider the fighting activity. Probably nobody ever really wants to fight; probably no person or animal ever wanted to fight but for a purpose. But it is recognized that men will fight for cause; they will at least fight incidentally. The early tribal fights of Indians were often of the nature of games—with incidental casualties, somewhat like those of football. Tournaments and wars were risky games, before the time of real efficiency in weapons. But let us admit that there is a strong susceptibility to combat for cause—a penchant for carrying on one's business by killing the other fellow. Does it follow that this human tendency must find expression in the slaughter of war? By no means. Substitute some activity that involves the enjoyable preliminary aspects of combat but is socially constructive. Indeed such civilization as we have owes no small part to the successful substitution of other objectives than those of historical warfare. One of the great wars of civilization was the "war" of the Panama Canal; another was the war against yellow fever; another, that waged by fire-fighting organizations. Raids into the enemy's territory have been carried on by Stefansson in the Arctic, by Dr. Schliemann in excavating the site of ancient Troy, and by Charles Evans Hughes in insurance investigations.

The evils of modern society represent misdirected energy. Social welfare depends upon the kind of response to environment and the right employment of natural tendencies and resources. To employ these aright requires some ingenuity, but not different in kind from that displayed by a skillful elementary school-teacher who takes numbers of unformed and misformed youngsters and finds acceptable vents for energies that, misdirected, would fill the juvenile courts with cases and their respective homes with confusion and despair. The playground bully is appointed the custodian of the laboratory, and this undesirable becomes the bulwark of law and order. To utilize the meanness of the individual for the good of the state, said Abraham Lincoln, is the purpose of politics. The social, industrial and economic problem is in essence merely the matter of setting up worthy aims and then securing the focusing of thought on the means to utilize constructively the abundant resources of the mental inheritance; likewise to stimulate the good will that will pursue them strenuously.

Primitive tendencies contain the makings of a high civilization. Man does not need to be re-created, to be made anew, to be something other than he is, or to be unnatural. His nature will do as it is. All that is necessary is for him to act differently, and this is comparatively easy. The farmer acts differently with tractor and gang plow than with an old-time crooked stick. But his motivation is about the same, only he is more intelligent through science; he has changed his methods, not his nature. Social organization and relationships are about where agriculture was in the crooked-stick stage. There are enough native resources, and energy, if efficiently applied, to realize the dreams of the ages. The supermen are here; every man is that potentially. Even the criminal prospect becomes a good citizen through method—what could not be done with the good citizen?

Unlike the Baltimore oriole with its inherited mechanism for building a particular type of nest and unlike all the lower animals that acquire their arts before they are born, man lacks almost wholly any precise mental specialization at birth. It is this fact that gives the measure of unique possibilities. In the sense that instinct is attributed to animals, man is almost without instincts. Instinctive tendencies he possesses, but of mechanically perfect responses to definite situations he is largely destitute. The infant sucks by instinct, but whether the adult will eat peas with a knife is a matter of education. Tendencies toward physical and mental activity are packed in the child's nervous system, but without conscious learning he would be at a disadvantage among creatures born with definite instincts. Learning is the greatest human fact. What shall be learned?

Any trait may be modified, and the instinctive tendencies may be swerved and attached to almost any objective. It is folly to assume that society is inherently committed to precise activities. Certainly there will always be marrying and giving in marriage, but whether by capture or by the squire depends. And whether woman is privileged to be beaten only with a stick "no thicker than a man's thumb," or is granted the ballot also depends. There is no social foreordination of details. The instinctive acquisitive tendency may always be expected to make its appearance. It is not necessary, however, that its form of expression shall be only in connection with privately amassed wealth. The tendency may show itself in pride of public ownership or in the accumulation of claims to public respect. Many a man indeed has transferred the ownership tendency to the storing of scientific facts or to the enlargement of his acquaintance with literature. The surgeon takes pride in the number of rare operations that he can lay claim to; this satisfies the property sense as truly as does a bank account. Many a man would rather have the largest fish to his credit than a successful angling for unearned increment on a vacant lot.

What form of expression the natural tendency and inborn capacity will take is always problematical. Under force of suggestion and formative influences the individual becomes a criminal or a saint, a nun or a mother of a family, a Quaker or a sword-flourisher, a cannibal or a vegetarian. No one is immune to the effects of his culture materials. The supreme strategy of civilization is to cut the channels through which energies may flow to acceptable ends. There is little in the raw materials of human nature that predetermines language, laws, customs and form of social practice and institution. Original nature can be readily adapted to the career of a pirate or that of an entomologist. Mankind is always in the making.

The throwing down of barriers among peoples by modern means of transportation and communication has caught the individual with a consciousness unready for fuller social relations. The tribal mind in a world made one by science is an anachronism. The individualistic viewpoint is nothing short of a nuisance under conditions that call for the psychology of the wide community. Stump-lot provincialism does not go well with radio and express trains. Legislation conceived in terms of the colonies and judicial decisions, in terms of the dissociated production of the one-man business, are evidences of the failure to acquire the requisite social mind. A bridge of sentiment and logic must be built from the insular, provincial viewpoint to cosmopolitanism. Narrow nationalism, sectarianism, and labor crafts organization alike attest the failure to reorganize thought on lines of greater inclusiveness. The balance between private and public interests, or the balance between the individual's welfare in private and public functions, is yet to be achieved.

Individualistic tendency, a response to a simple type of environment, is an impediment when society presents a complex environment of social relationships. In principle, the social problem to-day is one of the selection of responses; it invites to closer study of human resources and to a more canny and scientific procedure in utilizing these resources for civilization. Nearly everybody spends the early years of his life trying to see things less as they are than as he would like to see them. This attitude has been general during the years of our greatest scientific progress. Human nature has been idealized and seen through rose-colored lenses. The present disposition is rather toward impartial and realistic inventory. We expect fewer boys of our acquaintance to become presidents of the United States—and are less enthusiastic regarding the office itself. While the psychology of the morning after is a low-pressure affair, abasement that leads to minute self-study and practical reconstruction is really immensely hopeful. One thing is certain: Utopia, even the preservation of the existing level of welfare, will not be assured without a higher degree of planning and conscious effort. Accordingly, the scrutinizing of mental factors and resources available for social advance is of pressing importance.

Social problems to-day afford an unparalleled opportunity for further mental development. The multiform character of the demands made on the individual under modern social conditions is an outstanding fact. Here and there are individuals or groups not particularly subject to stimulating vicissitudes; but on the whole modern life is more stimulating and less settled to repose than life in former times. Too great demands thrown upon the individual overwhelm and destroy; or the mind balks in a protective stagnation like that of a horse on city streets. But the law of progress is, that only through stimulus and everchanging stimulus can mind be kept on its cosmic career of greater sweep and control.

The problems confronting modern society are unlimited. It would be unfortunate if end there were, for we keep alive by effort. Stimulus to invention and creative thought is needed. Social issues challenge and stimulate; they are what America was to Columbus. What then should be our attitude toward the problems that press upon us, even threatening to transcend power to solve? On no ground is there cause for lamentation. True, civilization is in the crucible. It always is. Mind has reached its present capabilities through analogous discipline in the past. New traits may be forced upon it—new sentiments, emotions, cautions, types of attention, new taboos. The mind of the coming social organization will differ from ours as ours differs from that of the theologians of the Middle Ages.

Custom, institutions, tradition, routine, history and precedent clamor for a definitive society, which would mean the end of adaptation and evolution. On the other hand, education, innovation, social experimentation, and the instinct of the pioneer are strong for the supreme act of adventure—the building of a society different from that ever known—and better.

Both by physical structure and brain development man has escaped fixedness of environment. New situations and problems have accompanied and affected his upward progression. Does fixedness of environment threaten his future? His substantial mastery of nature through science and invention might hint at a blind alley, but in the field of social and economic organization problems challenge. The world-wide emphasis upon education and the appearance of the concept of engineering in social relations indicate that equilibrium, static poise and incipient deterioration are not for our time. Fixedness of environment, though with it is associated arrest of development, tend to be sought as an end; but matters get out of hand and the conservative finds himself swept along by problems that will not be stayed. In the individual bosom opposed forces of progress and devolution contend. Ulysses and the Lotus-eaters are represented respectively by the ambition to achieve and the desire to leave things as they are.

IV

SOCIAL SIGNIFICANCE OF HABIT

Any consideration of the social utilization of our mental resources must necessarily take into account the reaction to environment represented by our habits. Habit and custom, like the law of gravitation, exert all-pervasive power. One often feels that the grip of social habit tends to be so complete as to yield but limited possibilities for the mobile factors of intelligence. Social welfare lies somewhere between the rigidities of custom and habitual performance, on the one hand, and the too free movement of the antennae of speculation and rationalism on the other. But for the present perhaps most of us would agree that society suffers rather especially from the rigidities of old use.

Habit is a stubborn force, though its tenacity is sometimes exaggerated. Bundles of habits though we are, yet the bundles need not of necessity always contain the same sticks. The value of habits is to enable us to do things more skillfully, in shorter time and with less effort and fatigue. The right hand writes smoothly, rapidly and with little effort and fatigue. The left hand traces one's name or writes a sentence only slowly, inexpertly, fatiguingly and with a taxing of attention.

Naturally, when once a habit has been laboriously formed and has become an easy and convenient accessory, we dislike to have it disturbed. Without an accumulation of pertinent habits no one would ever be able to have his consciousness and energies freed for use in novel and difficult situations. Knowing how to use pen or typewriter, the individual can give his whole mind to his thought and composition. Indeed, in the case of thought and composition even, habit may go far. It is said of Henry Ward Beecher that so fully had thought and composition gone down into lower nerve centers as habit, that after some of his most powerful speeches he himself knew little of what he had said; he was conscious only of attitude, emotion and purpose, and his habits of vocabulary, phrasing, and sentence and paragraph structure did the rest without involving definite consciousness. In other words, his consciousness took aim and his reflexes fired.

The sway of habit extends not only over physical acts, like writing with a pen, steering a motor car, skating, or pronouncing words, but extends as well over thought trends, emotional expression, association of ideas, and attitude and response to things generally. Without saying what my views are, I find myself possessed of certain thought and emotional habits toward Ralph Waldo Emerson, General Grant, P. T. Barnum, Thomas Hardy, Mrs. Eddy, the Negro, the Jew, the Pilgrim fathers, Thomas Jefferson, the high-wheel bicycle, and the Lewis and Clark expedition. Which is to say, the mind has acquired tendencies to react toward people and things in definite ways. Many such habits are loose and easily changed, while others are sometimes proudly declared to be good for "as long as I live," and are embedded in the physical structure of the brain.

Adaptability in one's lifetime would be a myth if habits could not be modified under pressure; we find in daily experience that even long-established habits may be superseded. Necessity is the antidote for habit. When one's telephone number is changed, one can forget the old number and form the habit of using the new number with no loss of time. The necessity of making this shift in habit dominates. Under conditions of no compulsion habits remain firmly seated. Exceptional circumstances rupture habits. A habit is said to be second nature; if so, a third and still other natures may be acquired under necessity. The habits that stay in place are those that represent the mechanics of everyday life and those that do not come in conflict with new necessities.

The most efficient type of person for social change is one who has a large and stable body of useful fundamental habits and who is comparatively free from habit, or is habitually elastic, where new responses are indicated. Under sanction of consistency, or creed, or historical party-platforms, or fear of what the neighbors will say, a large number of individuals prematurely harden into fogyism. Too much admiration of a fatuous sort has been lavished on being "always the same." It is very well to be always the same in "section one" of one's habits, but it is no less a virtue to be changeful in "section two," where to be changeful is to be more useful. Mobility is not only a delightful trait in people, especially elderly people, but is a valuable social resource. And let no one say that age is wholly opposed to new habits. Every reader can recall cases of men and women in the seventies and eighties who have open minds and take up without prejudice commendable novelty. The citizen who always does things the same way, always votes the same ticket, always reacts with the same saws and tales, always hangs his hat on the same hook and the same kind of hat at that, is far from exemplary. And no more exemplary, judged from the viewpoint of social purpose, is the man or profession strong on precedent. History affords fully as many examples of how not to do things as of the reverse. The historian may propagate undue reverence for the past by keeping before us matters that should be forgotten. If the yellowing volumes that bulge the walls of law schools were to be lost to mortal view—well, the world would manage to stagger along by getting up precedents founded on modern conditions.

At all events, it can be realized how one good custom can corrupt the world. People of middle age and beyond would be much more dynamic, if more stress were placed on the wisdom of keeping oneself constantly revised—if the inherited social tendency of bulldog conviction in the face of evidence were fairly discredited. Governed as we are by ideals, the value of publicity for the ideal of adaptability can scarcely be over-estimated. Indeed, in the instruction of children, whose plasticity is at par, the ideal of open-mindedness ought itself to be made a habit.

Education in ideals of habit revision, and of challenge of custom for cause, has large possibilities. The interrogatory state of mind can be promoted even as the static mind has been fostered by educational régimes. Instead of asking a pupil only for what he has learned from a book, he might at least be stimulated to questioning. The ultimate effect would be an attitude of inquiry, investigation and reflection. The personality-freeing kindergarten, devised by Froebel, a German, was banned in Germany on account of its inherent antagonism to subserviency, on the one hand, and autocratic domination on the other. There can be education for progress as definitely as there can be coaching for compliance with the *status quo*.

Along with specific education for mobility may be considered the progress-creating quality of various occupations. There are vocations in which survival waits on adaptability. The man who stands still in business to-day is left behind. In no part of modern society are there the tearless adieus to custom to be found in trade. Legislation, the courts, the church, the schools, all change, but tardily, as compared with business. No sooner does one automobile manufacturer produce a finished model than a competitor comes out with one having points of superiority, whereupon the first manufacturer is compelled to change his model. Business competition operating over large fields has done much to set up the modern type of progressive mind. Within the limits of his occupation the business man is often highly progressive. To what extent there is a transfer of training is another story. But the business office that daily registers price changes, market fluctuations, improvements in product, new inventions and competitors' strategies is one of the least conservative disciplines in the world. The modern business man's mind cannot stay made up. Deplore as we may the litter and wreckage of business, it has the merit of creating a yeasty condition of thought that has spelled the doom of such stagnation as prevailed in the long, uninteresting centuries before Francis Bacon.

The compelled elasticity of the business man waits only to be carried over to the wider field of social engineering and human betterment. The resourcefulness, the indomitable spirit, the challenging and even pugnacious frame of mind that have built railroads and monopolized coal, refined oil and exploited the public, are invaluable assets for social evolution. There is enough dynamic power and inventiveness, generated largely in business, to stage wonderland if directed to this end.

Consider the salesman. A perfect acquired egotism needs no formal complimentation. No missionary ever went forth more sure of the merits of his product, with more faith in the goods, than is possessed by the trained salesman. The salesman has been our most determined reformer—and the best paid. He has taken as his objective the timid retailer in a musty store and made a man of him—a business man. He has argued and cajoled, almost prayed; he has wheedled and bullied, poked in the ribs, treated to cigars and theater tickets. Finally, he has changed the habit-enveloped average man into a mood for accepting new ideas. Tremendous achievement! Millions of persons of the inertness and prideful torpor to which we are all prone has he made to see the merits of new things. The spirit for which the Hellenic Greeks are credited as the first to inoculate mankind with—the spirit of mental adventure—the salesman has spread to the ends of the earth and rendered in an epic of sales slips.

Moreover, he must be regarded along with peasants' revolts and Gracchian sacrifices as a factor in undermining despotism and freeing slaves; for he has demonstrated the brotherhood of man by recognizing the need of having pleased customers—an acid test for crowns and thrones. Not by express design nor by immediately humanitarian precept, not in sackcloth, has the salesman thus spread a religion, but he has nevertheless popularized a procedure for a happier world; for he has tried to please—serving both mammon and God. Which brings us nearer to Utopia.

One may fear that the salesman goes too far with his philosophy of "mixing" and of being a good fellow, and with his acquiescence in seeing his cherished views spurned without witnessing for them—when by witnessing he might lose a sale. There is a loss of the heroic in such restraint. But in any field the avoidance of minor collisions is often necessary to the securing of satisfactory final results.

Personal mobility and freedom from the cramp of too many and too completely fixed habits are promoted by occupations that present new problems and from day to day challenge ingenuity. The greatest progress may be expected in societies in which the daily demands of employment stimulate the mind through the presence of novel elements. A stable and unvarying employment tends to reduce life to a habit basis and therefore is inimical to social change. The choppy sea of modern business has the effect of developing versatile mariners and setting up attitudes favorable to constructive social effort. Likewise many of the professions and personally directed occupations throw the individual against emergencies and new demands, and accordingly conduce to initiative and vision as against social torpor, custom, institutionalism and tradition.

On the other hand, there are in modern industry a large number of employments that are essentially of routine character and that tend to deaden enterprise and promote timidity and dullness. In our shops, factories, and mines thousands are employed at tasks that are soon completely mastered and thereafter involve but a minimum of intelligence and conscious adaptation. Such jobs are ill devised for making inquiring, resourceful, and forward-looking citizens. One of the problems of social engineering is to provide suitable expression for persons working at mechanized tasks. Either a vent may be found in recreation and avocation, or relief may be afforded through increased use of machinery and the shifting of the worker from one job to another for the sake of a series of stimulating experiences.

Indeed, the possibilities of neutralizing the soporific quality of fixed employment by proceeding from one trade to another, from one job to another, from one position to another, from one specialization to another, deserve consideration. Personal and social welfare are threatened by the modern tendency to divide and subdivide labor, with corresponding limitation of individual experience. Vacations spent afield, cultural agencies brought to the factory door, travel and innovation in community and home life are possible for the salvaging of the worker. In many occupations the stimulating and intelligence-taxing demands are exhausted in a few years if not months. Upon such exhaustion the individual loses intensity of consciousness. His life becomes less a life and more of a mere animal-life existence. Faced with new demands, he is jarred into vivid consciousness again, and indeed may be quite rejuvenated by shock. Even calamity and death of close associates have been known to result in a new growth of personality and vigor in people quite advanced in years. Development is always compelled. A settled life seems to be a common ideal, whereas if there is anything that is deadly, it is the settled life. Many a man of forty would make much more a success of himself by "jumping his job." The peace of the tomb is prematurely achieved by such as get the problems of life tucked away and evade vicissitudes.

Any employment is stimulating for a while. A man who learns to lay shingles is distinctly being educated and made alert while in the apprentice stage. After the art has been fully acquired there is no more mental stimulus derived from laying shingles than there is for a horse in switching off flies with its tail. One of the most deadening influences is the unrelieved pursuit of an occupation. To have habits enough and not to have too many and to live in habit enough but not too much is well. It is particularly unfortunate from the social viewpoint when accredited mentors, like judges, hold their positions for life.

Analogous to the effects of too inclusive habit on the individual is the too close adherence to precedent in society. Invariableness in institutions and laws, in social procedure and community method, is no more admirable nor to be desired than ultra-stability in the individual. Early civilizations deified custom and repressed innovation. There is ever a tendency to strive for social inflexibility. Such endeavor discounts intelligence and conduces to degeneration and feebleness. Custom-breaking is as much of a virtue under justifying circumstances as is the reform of a drunkard. New paths should be sought for society not less than for the individual. Social experimentation may do for society what chemical experimentation has done for the dye industry and scientific agriculture. A good reason for some pieces of legislation is that they are experimental. Aversion to social experimentation is no better founded than the medieval horror of anatomatizing the human body in the interests of health; nor should the failure of a legislative experiment be a warning to all the ages not to try out new theories. If the business man can experiment in his advertising and the publisher with titles and bindings, there should be no initial aversion to working out social projects that have not been previously experimented with. Old technics of society, like old habits, should be assessed at true value; progress without the taking of chances and without adventuring is impossible. Practically every new law is an experiment. The frank adoption of the experimental attitude, with the circumspection of science, would do much to bring legislation and court decisions up to the level of the efficiency prevailing in laboratories and business organizations.

V

HABIT IN IDEAS—THE CONCEPT

The extent to which social adaptation may readily occur is measured to a large degree by the ease or difficulty of securing changes not only in habits but in general ideas or concepts. Indeed, our general ideas may be regarded as of the nature of memory habits or sets of mind, and therefore as promoting or opposing ready adaptations in the same manner as habits generally.

The general idea, or concept, represents the former experience of the individual and embodies a series of impressions. If an individual has come to have an established general idea regarding the proper limits of taxation or of the functions of municipalities, it becomes a matter of breaking habits to attempt to secure a modification of his point of view. The fact that opinions often rest on a basis of habit rather than of rationality is one that cannot happily be overlooked. We are all aware of how slow is the process of overcoming physical habit; the case is similar with reference to the meanings that the individual attaches by long wont to the terms in his vocabulary and the rules and principles by which he believes the world should be governed.

It should be noted, however, that change in general ideas, in opinions and conclusions, is possible. Electorates in various states are found to vote by majority one way one year and another way subsequently; a sufficient number of persons will change their minds to affect materially the results of elections. Apart from the influence upon elections of the first voters and of the deaths of voters, there is the pronounced factor of change of mind on the part of the voter. That people will change their minds admits of no denial; the habitual way of looking at things may be unseated in many instances; the accustomed concept may be modified and enlarged; recognition of new conditions affects opinion.

In view of the social implications of the concept, interest attaches to the processes by which one comes into possession of general ideas and convictions; it is also important to give heed to the possibility of impressing upon concepts a more social character. Some consideration of how the concept is formed and preserved is suggested by its significance in social program.

The concept or general idea originates in experience with things and cases that resemble one another. Its beginnings are seen in simple form in childhood. For example, a child sees a kitten for the first time. The kitten happens to be black. Blackness becomes a mark or quality or attribute of kitten till a white kitten is seen. Then kittens become either black or white, but having other traits also. Next others of still other color are observed, and finally the child's mind is forced to a concept of kitten that includes color but no color in particular. A general idea of kitten is achieved through acquaintance with various examples. Attributes other than color are also assimilated in a general idea, such as the possession of claws, mice-catching proclivities, night-prowling tendency and general contour and size. The child soon is able to classify a cat at sight. Cats are readily distinguished from dogs and goats. Later the child sees a tiger. The concept of cat has to expand to admit the idea of tiger; the child's mind comes to rest with a concept enlarged enough to include both cat and tiger. The achieving of a concept including both cat and tiger has entailed many readjustments. Upon achieving the wider concept the child has a more useful and effective intelligence than if he had stopped with the cat in one class and the tiger in a wholly different class. The differences between cat and cat, and between house-cats and tigers are not abandoned; but there is the useful concept of a class including cats and tigers.

This process of enlarging concepts goes forward in a multitude of experiences. The original and tentative concept is invariably wrong through inadequacy. Hence the young learner is forced to yield point after point as new examples force themselves upon his attention. A time comes, however, when one feels that he has cats and animals sufficiently well concepted, and he takes a rest; there is danger that he take a rest too soon.

In the "cat" case we have assumed that the concept was formed in early childhood, that there were enough cats to keep the concept growing; that the tiger was seen before the concept of cat became violently personal; and that nobody stood by to foozle intelligence by taboos and tales having a tendency to cause the receptive mind to behold a tiger with his stripes horizontal rather than around the body vertically. As a matter of fact children naturally perceive actual appearances and resemblances that adults may fail to note, because the former are freer from the limitation and distortion of views that instruction and words often promote.

The perceptions as well as concepts are influenced by the terms of their expression. Any one who has been taught early the words raccoon, bear, Airedale, woodchuck, chipmunk, gopher, gray squirrel, and baboon, will possibly see fewer resemblances among these animals than he would had he been taught names for all these having a common term, as dog. If the baboon were named tree-dog and the chipmunk called chattering-dog, and so on, the observer would perceive similarities that otherwise might go unnoticed or even be denied. Polonius saw first as a ship and then as a camel a cloud that Hamlet pointed out as such successively. The road to understanding is singularly set with signs capable of being misread or actually giving wrong directions.

The relation of words to accurate concepts is therefore one of some delicacy. How to guard against undue domination of the word, while utilizing to the full its unique economy, is a matter for consideration. For the moment a good strong word, spellable and mouthable, is adopted and its definition attached, there develops a tendency on the part of its possessor to cling to concept long after succeeding events have sucked away its substance. It may be that the lexicographers of the future will be found issuing bulletins warning against effete meanings and declaring extensions of significance. New conditions arise which are verily ignored or seen amiss because the most relevant word is preëmpted by a rooted meaning.

Vocabulary has scarcely kept pace with the need of saying things. The term "assault" refers to direct bodily attack. Now bodily damage not to be successfully distinguished from that inflicted by direct attack may be inflicted by selling some one a life-preserver that will not float. There is no word to label with equal opprobrium modernized, long distance assault and the assault of direct action, which may consist of a pulling of one's nose. Sin was a word; ah, there was a word. Are there phrases that truly convince the reader that to kill at a distance through defective workmanship is in the same class with common law murder? Or that to sell a stock that is worthless is to be conceived with entering through the coal chute? Where is the language that unveils the realities of petit larceny, grand larceny, and the separation on a large scale of investors' money from themselves?

The pitfall of the established concept is that it ignores nice distinctions that are oftentimes of the very substance of issues. The popular reaction to the words "in jail" is habitual and as such is undiscriminating. Whether honor or dishonor is to be attributed depends. St. Paul was in prison. Thoreau thought his own incarceration in Concord jail was rather a better state than being outside under the circumstances. There is a merited aversion to the thought of being sent to jail, but the unrevised concept may, at times, lead astray.

Practically every word bequeathed to us from the fathers has to be watched, or our thinking goes askew. Patriotism—holy word—and yet Dr. Johnson, in his time, essayed a fresh definition. Allowing a term to drag thought after it and accepting a word as a conclusive label is liable to lead us far from the essence of things. Especially in days of much reading and of impulsive response to headlines is there danger of unwittingly thinking evil and doing evil. It is no compliment to the circumspection of the citizen that it is currently held that the label in politics counts for more than the reality. Does the word Republican mean to-day what it meant in the days of Abraham Lincoln? It does not mean the same. Does it mean what it meant in the time of the French Revolution? Surely not. Yet the spell of the word is potent. It is convenient but unjustifiable to give words stereotyped meanings when used to apply to facts and situations which call for other terms or qualifying terms. Watchfulness in the use of terms applying to social phenomena and program is one of the most needed practices. The public should not be indulged in the impression that it is safely on the way to social welfare when a great body of terms looks one way and shoots another.

Definition is tedious, it is true. Tabloid news and radio do not affiliate with definition. But it is definition that has made science. Physics is a mass of exact definitions. He who learns chemistry learns, besides technic, definitions. Until social terms are defined with approximately the same exactness with which the chemist defines a substance or a reaction, and until some such respect is acquired for exact use of terms as every scientist regards as essential in his field of effort, social welfare and public administration will fail of their possibilities.

By too mechanical and unreflecting acceptance of words in lieu of perception of fitness for purported meaning, words become not aids and tools of thought, but disguises and false signals. Thought precedes language. Where language precedes thought—is adopted without perception into underlying facts—the proper function of speech fails and falsification appears. Somebody calls somebody else a scoundrel; the word scoundrel is easily repeated and clings to memory; scoundrel has an old, well established meaning. To be sure, it may not be the meaning that ought to be attached to the person labeled with the word. But it is easier to believe that Jones is a scoundrel, thus labeled, than to probe the facts of Jones' conduct or ascertain what his denouncer had in mind when he said scoundrel. It is objected that one cannot thus guard against the fallacy of words, that one cannot wait to ascertain the circumstances. But the practice of definition is commended.

The psychology of mechanical response to familiar words, such as fatherland, Jew, flivver, crown prince, protective tariff, mother-in-law, etc., is not essentially different from that of mechanical reaction to symbols. Flags have immense potency, whether carried for God and home and native land or for conquest and loot. It has been said that the rebellion of '61 might have succeeded if the confederate states had not adopted a new flag. In case either of words or symbols the fact of importance is that of the reality of their influence.

In the early years of one's life it is needful to revise and enlarge concepts freely. Plasticity of mind favors this and the demands of environment compel it. Knowledge is gained through personal experience and the annexation of other people's experience, and is filed away as general ideas or concepts. The exigencies of adjustment to surroundings dictate a certain flexibility in concepts in one's earlier years, a flexibility, however, that tends to pass away. Increasingly the mind tends to become made up, and increasingly the ideas that are stored away resist change. Teach the child aversion to pork, and it will take dieticians a long time to persuade to favorable consideration of pork chops; for pork has become something not conceivable as wholesome food. In thousands of instances the adult carries concepts that, whether properly formed or not, are habitual and definitive. Such finality of idea is not socially hopeful. In fact so firmly does the individual tend to become encrusted and bound by comparatively primitive concepts that institutional propaganda has always reached for the child.

The preforming of the individual's social concepts through pressure and propaganda in his childhood is, however, quite indefensible. The premature impressing of political, religious, and social concepts—where such concepts are debatable—is open to grave objection. To teach a child ideas that are to him at the time dogmatic and mind-closing is one of the ways to undo civilization. Even if parents have strong convictions, it is better to trust to ultimate rationality to bring the child to like convictions than to exert pressure. The child's mind should remain in a plastic state for arriving at concepts through enlarged experience. Provide evidence and culture materials but refrain from interference with the proper development of general ideas, should be the rule. I may be a firm believer in the government ownership of railroads, but it would be inexcusable in me to impress my concept of state function upon the immature. Such teachings would tend to make a youth a bigot. If my view of government ownership is worth anything, it will stand the test of social experience; the learner will presumably be controlled in his ultimate concepts by the available evidence and come to agree with me by coincidence; but if my view of state function proves to be erroneous he will at least be free from a false start. Similarly with religious and social views on controversial matters. If one is a Socialist, or Republican, or Methodist, or an Elk, he is not justified in putting the die on childhood. A large percentage of all the tedious and dogmatic rubbish in the world is with us because childhood has erroneously been regarded as the time to rivet on concepts. Childhood is the ever-recurring opportunity to roll away burdens of historical prejudice, social and sectarian fanaticisms and convictions for which evidence is lacking. The strongest evolutionist has no business to tell his eight-year-old son that evolution is ultimate fact. He should, on the other hand, direct the boy's mind to evidence, and let him come out ten years later where he may. It would not be such a calamity, if in the family various views were held, tentatively and until the third state of opinion, which is the agreement of the wise, were reached. It is a misconception of parental function for the heads of the family to dress up the children in the dogmas of years before. And there is no time like childhood to plant the thought that to make up one's mind in advance of evidence is not exactly the thing to do.

In dealing with phenomena that have no vital character, such as mathematical, the concept is definitive. But in the case of the phenomena under development general ideas must change with change. Moreover, in the case of vital phenomena, the evidence which supports a concept to-day may be affected by fresh evidence, whereupon there must ensue a revision of ideas.

It is not an accident that mobile intelligence has synchronized with the coming of biology. The doctrine of evolution has caused a perceptible tendency not to jump to positions from which there is no retreat. Nobody knows anything to-day with as much certainty as was displayed formerly by men who knew things that were not so. Nearly everybody to-day would admit possibility of error rather than go to the stake as a martyr. This may look like moral cowardice. Not so. It is the triumph of the sense of evidence.

Elasticity of concept is particularly appropriate for social relations. The ancient Jew had a clear idea of usury. Usury was holding up a fellow Jew. But it was quite right to take usury of the stranger. Here was a palpable case of arrested concept. Came one saying that the same moral laws should include all mankind. The brotherhood of man was a stirring and unwelcome concept of larger compass. Class justice, class legislation, class rule, class economics are proper concepts, provided the idea of class is inclusive. Nationalism is a finer concept if stretched to include the one nation of man. Class spirit in college is fine, provided it includes the freshmen as fellow creatures, and rival universities as institutions of learning. It has been said that no one amounts to anything until he forgets his college yell. Cases of restricted social concepts are many. The clan spirit of the Kentucky feudist represents arrested development; the true clan spirit, the socialized idea of kindred, stops not short of embracing surviving families in the same county, and the people of the commonwealth of Kentucky and even of these United States, including negroes, for their essential rights and fair play.

The socialized person is able to see the things that bind the many together as well as the things in which differences appear. Social vision is another name for the matured social concept. There is danger lest social concepts take fixed form with too limited connotations. Catholicity of view and readiness to modify one's opinions are of the essence of good citizenship and are an indispensable element for world citizenship.

Smug, provincial, and exclusively personal, modes of thought are out of keeping in times of the airplane, railroads, steamboats, the press, and the international organization of labor and scientists. It is the provincial and limited concept that provides submarines and Lewisite. The idea of universal brotherhood applied to armament would produce guns as destructive to the man firing as to the man fired at. A war rifle with safety at one end only is one of the least fitting symbols of equity

Progress comes with larger ideas of social organization and of justice; and collapse occurs through failure to adjust ideas to new developments of environment. Too restricted concepts were the psychological basis of the Civil War in America. The failure of George III and his ministers to adjust their concepts of colonial relations split the English-speaking world. In the appropriate expansion of concepts lies the world's hope. Distance, which has been practically overcome by transportation systems, exerts too great influence upon our ideas, for we as yet do not conceive of neighborhood in world terms.

Economic support for wider altruism is found in the bearing of remote societies upon local welfare. Backward groups tend to drag down education, health, and economic welfare throughout a whole country. The structure of trade and commerce is so complex and so essentially unified that no longer can one safely be indifferent to wages paid to miners two thousand miles away, or to the morale of the workers who contribute toward creamery butter. The standard of living and attitude of the Japanese toward birth-control have an international bearing. Tariff walls are erected in a spirit of disregard for other peoples. The concept of local independence and of disregard for the distant neighbor does not well conform to present facts of intercommunication and of modern business necessities.

Under limitations of concept there is a tendency to make too much of petty differences and to ignore the large bonds. Sometimes man and wife make this mistake; taxpayers have the habit too; wards and parts of cities misbehave thus, also large and small nations. Institutional Christianity has a record for magnifying unimportant differences. More can be had from coöperation than gained from selfish policy in the long run.

Wide social consciousness commends itself economically. But small part of the world's productivity is realized under present concepts of business and enterprise. There is no end of discord and waste. Under circumscribed notions in production and distribution large resources for social welfare remain but partly perceived or utilized.

Social engineering might assure a diffusion of prosperity never known before. Uncoördinated effort, staged under narrow and archaic concepts, stands in the way of rationalized and systematized social business with tenfold more power to provide goods and services. We should all be richer if, for example, the last bit of anarchy were removed from railroad construction and operation and the full possibilities of transportation were available for every hamlet in the land. Just as the concept of a highway as being four feet and eight and one-half inches wide limited the development of the railroad, so the conception of competing carriers limits railway service. The petty retailer who competes not in price but for trade would survive as a person under consolidated stores; he would survive in some capacity; he would probably share more in prosperity for there would be more to share.

The "boosting" efforts of small towns are commendable in that they represent an attitude preparatory to larger social undertakings. But community boosting is relatively helpless if narrowly conceived. The citizen's problems are in order of importance: international; national; state; and, lastly, county, city and local. But, quite naturally, influenced by the concrete, immediate and local, he thinks of them in reverse order. In a larger view, and as affecting his general interest the most important governing body for the citizen is the national congress, and the next is the state government, and so on down to the village board. Economic and legislative influences operating over wide areas deeply affect personal condition. As a self-contained organ of government, the local unit has ceased to have large significance.

VI

THE PSYCHOLOGY OF DEFENSE

In the lower range of animal economy defense is largely a matter of physical adaptation. Animals that are preyed upon are equipped with special means of protection—horns, poison-sacs, fangs, thick skin, quills, vile smell, tusks, protective masses of tissue, bony plates and shell armor. Means of flight are a means of safety, and long legs and muscles of wire enable the antelope and the rabbit to race to security. Protective coloration has marked survival value, as does also imitative structure, as in the case of the walking-stick insect, so closely resembling the twigs and needles of the pine branch to which it clings.

As mind is the organ of adaptation in man, the system of defenses is mainly mental. Tall stature and largeness of body and strength of muscle are but occasionally enlisted for defense. By use of physical auxiliaries and mental forces, the man of medium stature or less is substantially on a par with the giant or athlete. Indeed, by reason of necessity for refining his personal defenses, the small man may actually rise higher in the scale of security through his better conceived devices and improvisations. While bulk and bigness exert a perceptible social influence, the trend of defense and authority is toward control by mental forces quite apart from actual physical strength. In ordinary affairs, in the play of forces that determine the characteristic polity and adjustments in peace-time social organization, the advantage lies with those individuals and classes that are most highly specialized in mental means for getting what they want and avoiding what they do not want. Competition and defense are very generally and increasingly being moved upward to the mental plane.

The universal aspiration for education, if not for oneself then for one's children that they may be better fitted for the life struggle, is a recognition of the shifted plane of self-protection. The illiterate is in hopeless inferiority to the man who can read. The armed bandit with the strength of ten men and with ammunition for a hundred is a pigmy compared with the telegraph operator who helps put a noose of intelligence around the man killer. A man is beaten, he is conquered, he is routed, not physically but by statistics, logic, court decrees, underselling, loss of poise, ignorance, innuendo, wit, and propaganda. Defense is to-day a matter of psychology; even war has succumbed to the superior factor of mental as contrasted with physical potentiality.

The primitive mental defense is falsehood. Instinctively the child deceives; when in doubt of policy the child often turns to untruth. The tendency may indeed be superseded within limits by the attaching of penalties and rewards but of the original response there can be no doubt. Early moralists held up their hands in horror over this supposedly iniquitous phenomenon and regarded it as clinching proof of the original depravity of human nature. Little men and little women were discovered to be just naturally "little liars." Threatened by dangers from the adult world that towers physically over his low stature, the child takes to falsehood instead of flight, instead of use of teeth or claws, vicious expectoration or digging in. He instinctively utilizes—so great a step does human evolution represent above the animal—his resources of deception. Deception is nature's shock absorber. It is biologically as great an advance over the corporeal defenses of the animals as the tractor-drawn gang-plow is an improvement over the forked stick of the Egyptians.

Worthy to be mentioned along with falsehood as a cautious tendency, and like falsehood in having a certain significance for constructive social psychology, is the defense which consists of taking the back seat. If he who runs away is safe, so also is he comparatively who takes a back seat or sits with his back to the wall. When an audience assembles there will ordinarily be a drift of individuals around the fringe of the room unless the entertainment is to consist of something to be seen and familiar through repute. The lecturer must often pray that his audience will move forward and fill up the unoccupied seats near the front. The peripheral tendencies of popular audiences have not escaped notice.

Here we have the psychology of the animal that fears an inclosure; it is the fear of being trapped. A certain ex-miner from the once wild west, on visiting his eastern relatives, was observed never to take a chair that was not tight on the wall. He had contracted the habit while living under frontier conditions, and preferred to have no chance of enemy attack from the rear.

Flee from the strange, or if drawing near, draw not too near; and if fairly faced, lie, and lie abundantly—these reactions are not of yesterday's growth.

Instead of the defenses of falsehood, retreat and taking the back seat, evasion is a common ruse. In the psychological sense evasion extends to the setting up of illusions and self-deception. Or evasion may take the form of a selection of interests that minimize the possibility of conflict. Thus art and music are refuges in an autocratic society. It is not surprising that these have reached high development in monarchies, in which constructive effort and philosophizing along social lines have been banned, with Siberias in the background. In times past a multitude of thinkers and men of parts have illustrated the psychology of evasion by devoting themselves to labors that had a minimum of potentiality for conflict.

Not alone by restraint from possible fields for employment of energies, but also in the vision of alluring worlds does the psychology of evasion disclose itself. Hans Christian Andersen substituted a fairyland for the real world of childhood, evading the actualities for which he was so little adapted. The downtrodden classes of the Roman empire accepted Christianity the more readily for its affording an avenue of escape into a world in which the bitter struggle of living was to be forever removed. The most unsuccessful and deprived are frequently those who dream most dreams and see most visions. The minds of dwarf, cripple, hunchback and chronic invalid are rich in evasions and cushioned with illusions. With the exhaustion of ordinary and real methods of defense, the individual flees to unreality and air castles. In time of calamity and war the appeal to charms and luck, to miracle and myth, increases. The farmer who is least consistently scientific is likely to be most devoted to "moon" farming and most conscious of the luck of seasons. By attaching results to inexplicable causes he thus saves his face. The Freudians declare that insanity itself is an organic adjustment of evasion. The victim of irreparable loss flees from himself and "becomes" by the rôle or route of insanity, the King of Norway or the great Napoleon. Reality too terrible to be faced becomes thus unreality, and unreality becomes the seeming real.

It is evident that the psychology of evasion is at war with social progress. Whatever mires mind in illusion and upholsters it with the fanciful is directly opposed to the making of a better real world. It is not an accident that with the more forceful efforts on the part of the church to reform modern evil conditions, there has ensued a notable lessening of emphasis upon dogma and future bliss. Dynamic individuals address themselves to immediate improvements. Material success is inversely related to certain brands of theology. With prosperity invariably comes a loss of the religious fervor related to remote objectives, for there is less tendency to evade what the day and hour present.

The presence of great poverty, of war and revolution, of industrial anarchy, is fraught with danger lest life slither to illusion through despair rather than gird up its loins. There comes a time in the life of the individual when he no longer tries to swim; he submerges. The spirit of society must be that of practicality and hopefulness, or society fails. An amount of misery may prove stimulating; but increase that amount beyond a certain limit and only decay may be expected. The most energizing mood is that of confidence born of success. There is no class so valueless for social reconstruction and abiding welfare as the class that is habituated to misery. The slums of city and country afford little material for building a better society. Long continued abasement is of little promise. It is important to society that welfare be general, that the poor should not always be with us.

A refinement of defense appears in keeping one's thoughts to himself. Avoidance of telling the whole truth and nothing but the truth serves notably for survival purposes, and escapes the burden on memory of successful dispensing lies. The morality of concealment is a stage higher than that of even the "white lie." A large part of trade rests upon concealment. The buyer knows that a tract of farm land is to be sought as golf links; the farmer is permitted to remain in ignorance of this important fact until he has signed the deed. This is "good business." The goodness of business is not inconsistent with "doing" the other fellow by keeping him in the dark. The automobile dealer markets the older model, keeping discreetly silent on improvements about to appear. If trade were to see the elimination of all deceptions and concealments, some of us would scarcely know how to do business. Trade is thus vastly lower in evolution toward full veracity than is science, which is truth without fear or favor. In the social renovation, for which science is laying the foundation, trade may approximate if indeed not fully realize the same loyalty to truth to which we are accustomed in the laboratory. The big "strikes" in the business world will possibly some day be squarely bottomed on absolute candor—scientific method. As yet few have the nerve to be scientifically honest in business, but are "law honest" or are constantly being forced by law into an acceptably ethical attitude.

The evolution of defense carries over to the use of imagination and intuition for grasping what is in the other person's mind. As long as self-protection is limited to the doing of something to meet overt attack, there is obvious disadvantage. The best defense is often correct anticipation. The individual is relatively defenseless until he can see what is going on in the mind that he encounters, until he can judge motives, until he sees what is to happen before it happens. The pugilist gets a "nose" who waits to see a blow in the air, before he sees it in his opponent's mind. Under modern conditions the mind is forced to organize for penetrating into what others know and what they will do; hence the emphasis upon psychology and character analysis.

It is idle to hope that pickerel will ever cease from eating minnows, or that superior intelligence will not take some toll from inferior; this would be too much to expect. Life struggle in human society may indeed be raised above the level of competition for plain subsistence. Bread for all may come to be an accomplished fact. But advantage seeking will none the less obtain, perhaps intensify. Honors, place, repute, distinctions, immunities, and power are high substitutes for means of subsistence, but are in true biological sequence with the struggle of two dogs for sole possession of a single bone.

Superior intelligence tends to take advantage of inferior intelligence; the only abiding protection is in the development of mental tactics of defense. Though society without exploitation is unthinkable, such exploitation by superior of inferior intelligence need not be immobile and rooted in social classes. Constitutional safeguards may be provided. By more agile defenses and by specialized leadership class lines stretch and break. Fixedness of individual status, except as children are ever dominated by their elders, is not a foregone conclusion. The mistress and maid are both in turn exploiter and exploited; the wits that are sharpest on the issue determine the respective rôles. In Barrie's *The Admirable Crichton* the butler was an inferior when the family he served was in its English setting, but he in turn, under different circumstances, became a master when on the sea-girt island with the patrician family that lacked practical knowledge. The war of wits never knows an armistice; and outside of one's knowledge one is helpless.

Democracy is identified with distribution of opportunities for information and intelligence. Given free play in opportunities, the individual has democracy indeed. Social contrast and oppression have been associated with the device of depriving the people of thought-materials or with that of controlling minds through fictions and class taboos. What would autocracy be without illiteracy or special cultures of prejudice? Information and catholic culture are incompatible with the existence of submerged classes. The recipe for the security of despotism is popular ignorance and moth-like tropism toward the sun of royalty. Class advantage is least possible with uncontrolled press, church and school. In England the political ministry appoints the bishops of the established church, and the landlord owns the vicar. In pre-war Germany the clergy had no thoughts that were not visaed. The liberating of the mind to truth and science is the only defensible function on the part of cultural agencies; and when any of these agencies holds a brief for the landlord class or the monarchical group or the moneyed interests, the mental energy of the people is misdirected and betrayed, and civilization hangs on by an eyelash. The full intelligence of the people, the intellectual resources of the whole people, is the greatest assurance of general welfare, including ultimately, that of those who clutch privilege and fear its loss.

While propaganda has gained recent prominence to secure warlike responses and is increasingly employed for purposes requiring mass opinion, it is no new thing in the world. Propaganda is as old as society. There was never a time when propaganda was not employed. The distinction attaching to present-day propaganda is quantitative rather than qualitative. Propaganda is twin brother to advertising, but goes beyond commercial advertising in that control of fundamental attitudes on great issues is sought, and not infrequently for no perceptible benefit to the people whose sentiments are thus commandeered and dominated.

Just as psychological salesmanship—the refined hypnotism of the market—has caught the ordinary buyer unprepared in a counter-psychology of resistance, so propaganda has developed more fully than defensive tactics on the part of the public. The psychology of resistance is in its infancy. Hence the consumer is frequently no match for the seller and the voter is a lamb before the all-the-year publicity service of the bureau of propaganda.

There is valid propaganda and objectionable propaganda, just as there is legitimate and illegitimate salesmanship. It is no small service when the salesman promotes the purchase of goods that are within the buyer's purse and effects an upward thrust on the plane of living and intelligence. But there is likewise a salesmanship that is nothing short of a psychological and economic raid. With propaganda it is likewise. Progress is associated with propaganda; but, on the other hand, there is not a shady policy or selfish project that does not hope to use propaganda as a narcotic. The extent of governmental and private use of propaganda is strong evidence of the arrival of society at a level characterized by mental rather than physical strife. From now on it is the battle of ideas; an environment has been established wherein the mobilization of ideas and psychological strategy are outstanding features.

The ordinary man, not yet armored against propaganda, succumbs like an Eskimo to measles. His actual government, never of high visibility, becomes an invisible government. He learns what he is told and he is told what others think he should be told, for their interests. Immune from physical violence through his courts and constables, he is psychologically assaulted and ravaged with impunity. Thus he will be found enthusiastically supporting campaigns aimed at his own subversion, voting against his own interest, bawling down his best defenders and worshiping the devil. He thinks, when he thinks, on the ideas and facts presented. The control of his thought materials, through selection and interpretation, is accordingly a most effectual control over his convictions and conduct. Suffering from effects of propaganda the sufferer is the last to admit that he is sick; he feels well. The sensations that the propaganda germ set up have the seeming authenticity of normalcy. The victim of propaganda is myopic without knowing it, having no idea of how lenses would improve his vision.

The primary remedy against subversive propaganda is for the citizen to know who says what. In one's daily dealings it makes a difference who says a thing. A land agent will see qualities of soil and beauties of landscape that might escape the ordinary observer. The fallibility is known, and there is locally an allowance made for overstatement. It is usual to weigh words with motives in the small circle of acquaintanceship. The questioning of motives, however disparaged, is the first requisite for successful adjustment in one's own neighborhood. Not to scrutinize motives is to repudiate cause and effect.

But in the wider circle of political and economic affairs like regard for motives is less prompted and less practicable. The remote source of opinion is endowed with a disinterestedness not attributed to the man around the corner. The panegyric on war is reverently perused with no thought of the chortling of the powder manufacturer. The ukase of fashion to wear more buttons is received with a pupil-like docility that would not be extended to a suggestion of like import from the next-door neighbor. Distance not only lends enchantment—it convinces. Anonymous advice has a clear lead over that from the reputable local authority. Propaganda from invisible and seemingly impersonal sources accordingly has a peculiar prestige and sanctity. The tendency to tolerate a wonderland where all the usual laws and phenomena are transcended, falls in with the designs of propaganda.

The citizen needs to be as skeptical of sources as is the competent historian or the scientist. The "doubting Thomas" should not be the exception but the rule. The results upon journalism would be galvanic and most constructive for social well-being. One might well finish every newspaper paragraph with a question mark, not that every paragraph is unreliable, but by way of training for keeping off the rocks of occasional doctored news and inspired interpretation. "Prove all things," is peculiarly applicable to articles published in the heat of conflict and in journals top-heavy with advertising. The gross control of news and editorial by advertisers may be unusual; but who would deny that the whole glacier-like influence of the advertising is to limit the intellectual value of the press? Publications read by the most millions are often essentially advertising mediums and should be so regarded.

Anonymity contributes to the tactics of propaganda. We can have no objection to an article extolling the use of beer as a medicine if we know the writer owns a brewery. It is the mass of articles camouflaged as scientific or disinterested that perverts public intelligence most seriously. We do not regard with favor commercial products that do not carry the maker's name. Yet the thought products that go into the mental assimilation of the people are not similarly referable to the actual sources. The signing of articles is desirable—and more than that, for signatures are inconclusive evidence of motive—there should be disclosure of the economic or political origin. An importer writes or hires a man to write for free trade. We may accept the argument; but the chances of being misled are reduced if we know what interest is back of the article. Here is a powder manufacturer who believes in the evoking of superior moral qualities by blowing holes through people one has not met before. Very well; some may agree with him; give him his say anyhow. But let him not hide behind a clergyman, or buy an editor by an advertising contract. The same authenticity in mental foods that we have in other foods is desirable—name of the beneficial owner and exact nature of contents of the package. The direct linking of utterance with person and interest is a desideratum. Find the man, is the idea; see how he secures his income; listen to him though he is a homicide preaching against jails; but let us no longer be in doubt as to motives, nor should we assume that the man who writes from selfish interest may not be serving the public interest too; let us be open-minded.

Correlated with the idea of reliable information and ascertained sources of thought-materials is the ideal of insuring conditions for free speech. Only belated progress has been made toward endowing the employee with the attributes of free citizenship. Every citizen has a right to vote for whom he pleases, to espouse any political or economic theory—free speech being guaranteed by federal constitution—and criticize public officials, who are legally his servants. Does the employee have the right to exercise his rights? Legally, yes; practically, not always.

Originally the economic subordinate was kept where others thought he belonged by denying him the ballot. Then he achieved the ballot; thereafter the landlord or employer's agent looked over his shoulder when he voted. So the ballot was a scrap of paper. Then came the Australian ballot—the greatest contribution to the mechanics of democracy ever devised.

This emancipated the social subordinate. Secret voting, which is contemplated by the secret ballot, is the sheet anchor of democracy. The voter who thinks the secrecy of the ballot is being violated may attack such violation successfully without revealing necessarily how he votes. He is assured of the unique freedom of being able to vote as he will without detection. Without this freedom there can be no political democracy. This is the cornerstone.

It only remains to carry the secret ballot further.

It should be available for expression of preferences on a wider range of public questions, as for example, a declaration of war and major enactments of legislation before such go into effect. But perhaps the greatest remaining usefulness of the secret vote is to be found in its exercise in a multitude of quasi-public situations where the psychology of aggressive leadership threatens the sincere expression of convictions. The chairman of a meeting, in thousands of instances where public sentiment is polled, may dominate and evoke a perverted expression of views. Job fear, fear of loss of trade, and apprehension as to how an open vote for or against will be regarded, commonly have the effect of a miscarriage of intelligence. In committee meetings, clubs and local organizations, publicity of voting is a restraint. The psychology of the individual in such groups is one thing and his psychology under the secret ballot is another. Openly voting, his concern is how others will regard him, how he will be affected, as by scorn or trouble-making. Voting secretly, his freer self finds expression. In Mark Twain's *The Mysterious Stranger* only two or three of the sixty or more who stoned a woman to death were interested to have her die. All the others joined through fear to be in a minority.

The very foundation of democracy and stable popular government rests upon the secret ballot and especially in the extension of this to weekly and daily use in the frequent local and institutional meetings in every municipality, school district, and community. The secret ballot, for all matters likely to involve job fear and the like, should be a matter of course.

True, the secret ballot is a thing for the weak. Free and open expression is a much nobler concept than furtive voting. But heaven is not reached at a single bound. The right to discuss public policies and public men, the voter's agents, is assured; it is violated only in practice.

The employee has the secret ballot; what more should he want? All the historical and logical considerations which convince that the stability of society rests on free intelligence functioning for general welfare, declare for free speech—for the composite intelligence built up when all speak freely even if some utter nonsense. Now the employer and employee may think differently; they are apt to. It is hard for the employer to realize that free speech is a blessing to society, in the long run, and hard to check an impulse to dismiss the employee who differs with him on the tariff on wool. Here is the employee who has views on labor and capital. Here is a governmental employee who criticizes the governor. Shall it be permitted? Millions of men and women are now within the working forces of government and business corporations. The job web is as wide as society. In the nature of things must the loyalty of the employee to the employer take precedence over his interest in the general welfare and stop his mouth? The tradition of democratic freedom of speech grew up when the jobs were numerically insignificant. When private corporations count their employees by thousands and the federal government employs an army of men, inquiry is in point touching the civic freedom and potentialities of these great numbers of workers.

To be a good citizen implies civic activity, and such is unthinkable without freedom to discuss issues, take part in campaigns, and comment favorably or unfavorably upon the government, which derives its lawful powers from the will of the people. To the extent to which employment silences the employee, whether he be a private or a public employee, it is in conflict with the welfare of the state. The remedy lies in guaranties of tenure as against loss of place for exercising civic rights. It is no less duress to attack the citizen economically for exercise of civic rights than for him to be attacked physically for the same cause, which no government would tolerate. When the employer is the government, it is difficult to see any distinction between summary removal for exercising civic rights and such coercion when applied by the private employer. No employer can be fairly said to buy the opinion and political life of the individual when buying his labor power. The very existence of democracy depends upon the widespread cultivation of political intelligence. There is a duty resting upon every voter not only to vote but to seek by every means to enlarge his knowledge of public issues and the industrial and economic problems now so largely identified with public affairs. To be an intelligent citizen without freedom to shape public opinion and frame resolutions, or run for office or sit on the platform at a political meeting, is a contradiction in terms. There is urgent need of meeting the requirements of citizenship. Through more rigid and comprehensive corrupt practice acts and through more complete organization of employees to protect their constitutional rights as citizens, the dismissal of men for overt citizenship should be made to take its place with relics of the past.

VII

THE BASIS OF COÖPERATION

Picture a boat, far from shore, containing several men threatened with drowning. No one man can get to shore without aiding the others to land as well. Each man would be willing to be the only survivor if only one were to survive. There is discord and harmony, "private property" and community effort. The major interest is that of making a successful passage to shore, and this interest welds all muscles into one motive force. Men tend to "do" one another, but they will also coöperate on a pinch.

There can be no social advancement, no civilization, without coöperative effort. If coöperation is not possible, civilization is not possible. There will be more coöperation in the future—partly conscious and partly in fact only, as in the coöperation of the ranchman and the shoe manufacturer, who have not the full consciousness and purpose of coöperation. Deliberate and planned coöperation is illustrated in municipal waterworks, state highway construction and in community effort and team work of any kind.

Coöperation works when each coöperator thinks he can get more for himself through working with others than alone; this is the basis for coöperation. A vision of advantage is pitted against the disorganizing factors of irritations and jealousies.

Envy and jealousy are largely phenomena within the class. The resentments from class to class are as nothing to those among individuals within classes—among individuals of local association. The question of who shall be first among equals is solved with greater difficulty than who shall be first when there is a higher class to pick from, or when the class embraces individuals not of intimate acquaintance. Oftentimes local discords can be alleviated only by bringing in a stranger. It is hard to believe that a familiar acquaintance and competitor for local repute can possess the qualifications for important office. Aside from persistent wariness lest rivals succeed, there is the besetting myth that the distant is superior. Amateur stockmen send to distant points for breeding animals though the next ranch may have their superiors; and the amateur gardener rarely thinks of saving seed from his own crops, that coming by mail being naïvely assumed to be better.

Democracy has even attempted preposterously to level, if not by denying elevation, then by rotation of office. Surely every citizen is entitled to hold office, from which axiom arises change of personnel and the diffusion of opportunities to do things inexpertly. The craving for office, while adjusting the balance of titular equality, does indeed often rotate efficiency out and inefficiency in.

The hatreds and jealousies of democracy yield to the sense of impending calamity or the clearer vision of benefits from joint action. Bickerings in the family, in the social group, in the civic organization, vanish under threat of harm. Identify public and coöperative effort with security and survival, charge public affairs with weightier import, and the sensibilities of rivalry are quieted. The unifying effect of great distress is analogous to that revealed when private welfare is seen to be momentously related to the proper conduct of public business.

Individualistic commercialism sprouts its growth of coöperative psychology. The emphasis upon service to the buyer, an emphasis bobbing about like a cork on the competitive sea, testifies to the social vacuum yet to be filled by coöperation. The dealer cannot live to himself alone. He must even pull with others—other dealers and his customers—to get to shore. A distinct kindliness and fraternity blossoms in trade, a forerunner of more systematized and perfect coöperation. Should tradesmen stop competing in prices and take to competing in good will and amenities to customers, the change though no relief to pocketbooks, would be of great social promise. The slogan of service, heard in the market place for some years back, is auspicious. It connotes a wider social consciousness and a sense of interdependence; it bespeaks a recognition of the good of all in the good of each and the prosperity of each in the prosperity of all. The psychological basis is being laid thus for larger political, social and economic synthesis.

Modern industry has been accompanied by a tendency toward coöperative consumption of surplus private wealth. The age of industrialism has become the age of large giving. Leaving aside the ethics of accumulation and the deficiencies of philanthropic purpose and method, the fact stands clear that wealth is conceived of increasingly in terms of public welfare. Its social origin and social utilization are distinctly implied by the colossal gifts and returns of money to common and public uses. In logical sequence follow a greater formal and conscious coöperation in the production of wealth and a greater legislative or popular direction of its distribution and use. The violent individualist and the determined socialist are really not far apart except in vocabulary. The recognition that the social body is one and we are all of that body may be denied as a theory, but it is accepted as a fact generally, though with differing states of mind and varied reservations.

Coöperation succeeds in so far as it secures for the individual things that alone he could not secure. It fails to interest the individual who will lose more than he will gain by it. Few can ever be as interested in getting things for the public as for themselves. Hence any system that flouts private property completely cannot stand. The case against capitalism is that it trespasses far upon private property, for there are great numbers who are unable to possess enough private property to satisfy distinctly personal as contrasted with public needs. If capitalism ever goes upon the rocks, it will be because it has trifled too much with the private property sense. As between no private property and public ownership the voter will choose public ownership every time. But at the bottom his choice is for private property, though not with unwillingness to see others enjoy private property. The barrier between capitalism and social ownership in its most sweeping form is the popular faith in the possibility of each person's securing a good share of private property himself; let this faith waver and strange things might happen.

It remains to be seen how fully the property sense may be satisfied by an undivided share in, say, a public library as contrasted with money in the bank to buy books. It is possible that the amount of free money the citizens would be content with might be small indeed, provided public utilities abounded on every hand. It was Thoreau who found it unnecessary to buy a farm for scenery when he could look at farms without owning them. With growth of socialized utilities it is quite possible that the sense of private property would be adequately gratified with fortunes that would look small at the present time. Balzac, in *Cousin Pons,* wrote satirically of the gilding of the gas-lamps in the Place de la Concorde to console the poor man for his poverty by reminding him that he was rich as a citizen.

Close attention to immediate results is opposed to the state of mind required for successful coöperation. Many of the advantages procurable through social big business cannot be realized at once. The need of exercising some imagination for the anticipation of benefits is a check on popular interest in the larger coördinations for social program. It is hard to interest people in things they cannot see and in matters that concern the future. Consider the indifference in this country to the conservation of forests and other natural resources. Citizens rally to fight fires but tend to be indifferent in regard to fire prevention. Once an epidemic of disease appears, active measures are taken; but social coöperation for preventive medicine is less readily brought about. It is the idealistic and imaginative who see most in coöperation. The individual who has but flighty attention and whose mind is uncomfortable in tracing relations is accordingly but slightly qualified for coöperation in its many forms; and essential dividends from social effort have not the satisfying tangibility of the cash rebate.

A certain weakness of coöperation is shown in the compensation of public servants. Coöperative enterprise to be successful needs, of course, as highly qualified staffs as are employed in private business. Democracy is not privileged to get along with inferior agents. To secure highly efficient agents rewards must be offered equivalent to those afforded by private employment. Such compensation is unusual and is attended by distinct pain on the part of citizens who would secure high skill at a unique discount. Hence it is that generally public and coöperative affairs are directly administered by men of ability who give a part-time service to the public or by persons not comparing favorably in resourcefulness and technical training with persons in corresponding activities in private business. In hundreds of communities will be found men drawing salaries from private employers much larger than any paid by the same communities to their most highly compensated civic employees. In the unequal contest public business accordingly suffers. In the final analysis all salaries, whether in public or private business, are socially derived. The citizen, however, tends to be singularly alert and thrifty, in paying his own experts, singularly given to uneconomical economy in communal affairs.

If the downtrodden turn to coöperation for security, no less so may the privileged. A very large part of the work for social amelioration has been inaugurated and carried forward by persons whose immediate needs would not seem to be served by such altruism. The spirit of social adventure is no doubt far more potent in the classes than in the masses. Imagination, forcefulness, inquiry, sympathy—these are not of plebeian character. The noblest roll of history is that of names of well-placed individuals who have felt the common lot and striven to uplift. Their stake has been the clearing of their souls from injustice, and the luxury of constructive idealism.

Economic privilege has also its essential interest in popular welfare. The monopolist cannot prosper without a market. Poverty beyond limits is a menacing condition even to those who are immediately immune. The large operations of business presuppose a degree of general prosperity.

One of the reasons most frequently cited for private as contrasted with public business is that individual initiative would tend to disappear with any considerable expansion of the latter. It is likely that personal initiative will always find avenues of expression. Initiative might merely be shifted to new fields. Public and private success are not mutually exclusive; both have expanding and largely nonconflicting orbits. The resourceful individual can always do something else. Loss of initiative would be one of the most irreparable of losses. Persons urging greater social coöperation as well as those who oppose it unite in insistence upon the need of free play for initiative. The merits of social programs must be judged according to effects upon initiative. There are those who conceive a larger field for initiative under an economic system less individualistic than that at present operative.

VIII

THE PSYCHOLOGY OF PUBLIC BUSINESS

It is assumed that civic and social progress involves wider coöperative effort and a relative increase in public as contrasted with private business. The trend of modern government is toward expansion of function, which touches increasingly industrial and economic relations.

There was a time when the resident of a city, such as London, hired guards for his body and his warehouse and lighted the street in front of his premises—when he was his own police and street-lighting department. He was also his own fire department and sanitary expert. The past century has witnessed the steady augmentation of public business. An increasing number of employees are attached to government; service offices multiply, and the citizen tends ever to get more things for himself by utilizing the coöperative mechanism of the state. Governmental regulation for protective purposes obtains where forthright ownership and monopoly have not become seated in government. In the sharp contest between public and private ownership and control, the decisions fall to socialization. The tendency for peoples under modern conditions to develop the coöperative agency of the state is an outstanding phenomenon. To mention a few examples of extension of governmental function as revealed by federal legislation: the interstate commerce act; the Sherman anti-trust law; the anti-child labor law; the farm loan act; the federal trade commission law; the Clayton act; rural free delivery of mails; the parcels post; activities of the department of agriculture; the pure food and drugs act; the Smith-Hughes educational act; the Muscle Shoals project. In states; such projects as the New York barge canal, public warehouses in Louisiana, state fire insurance of public buildings in South Carolina, state mining of coal for public uses in South Dakota, state elevators and state bank in North Dakota. In foreign countries, notably in Australasia and Germany, state enterprise has shown vigorous growth. Municipalities the world over show similar enlargement of function. There are community playgrounds and parks, libraries, water systems, food inspection, vacation schools and street railway lines. Within the school are the free dental clinic, and hammers and saws in the manual training department bought with tax money and owned by the community for a community workshop.

Yet with all the tendency toward substantial socialization, and with the accumulating evidence that social welfare involves such increase of socialization, there remain states of mind in the citizen body that seem to threaten the success of public business. It is an open question whether the citizen is going to be adequate for upholding an elaborate structure of public business.

There is, first of all, the question as to whether the citizenship can be kept informed. In case the government, which is the agent of the citizen in democratic theory, becomes walled off by itself and is virtually inscrutable to the citizen, the probability of vicious bureaucracy and perversion is obvious. Every official, board, committee, staff, court and cabinet tends to magnify office and reach for power. Unchecked and unwatched officialdom undoubtedly, everywhere, and at all times, tends to grow beyond proper limits. The seeds of autocracy are present in the most hopefully constituted instrumentalities of democracy. A strict holding to account and daylight openness of procedure and purpose are needful lest the agent become principal, lest corruption creep in and privilege and profit take the place of service to the state.

Two things are needful: first, a manageable system of reporting to citizens, and, secondly, a workable system by which the civic body can instruct its agents. In both of these particulars improvement is imperative if modern government is not to prove disappointing or the prelude to collapse.

In regard to the first, what does the citizen authentically know about the official conduct of his agents in congress, in state legislatures, in municipal bodies? What are the means by which information is provided? The opacity and inadequacy of the agent's reports to his principal, the citizen, are notorious. The other side of the moon is about as visible as the official conduct of a very large number of persons employed in government. This condition goes ill with democratic theory. Perhaps the theory is wrong, then what better theory? It is, however, demonstrated beyond debate that it is possible to fool most of the people most of the time. The official in a republic may live as in the seclusion of a hidden cave, and when put on the defensive has rich resources for "passing the buck." Any business man who turned his agents loose with power to act would regret it. The voter selects his agents but has to be a detective to follow what they do. The art of reporting on public business for the benefit of the citizen-principal may fairly be said to be underdeveloped.

On the other hand, the citizen, ostensibly principal, with power to instruct his agents, the office-holders, has but singularly limited means of making his agents hear. The agents are often honestly unable to hear from their principals, who vote infrequently and in such murky form of expression that days and days are spent after elections by the newspapers in trying to see what the elections indicated by way of policy. Parties go into power mystified as to what they are expected to do. Analyzing the election returns becomes a brain-wrecking exercise in the unknowable. It often takes years to develop a tentatively right guess as to what the voters meant by this majority or that slump.

In view of the wonderful efficiency of communication in private affairs, as illustrated, for example, in the facility by which one calls up the grocer over the telephone and is understood, the inability of electorates to make their representatives understand by ballot is passing strange. Perhaps the form of the ballot is at fault or the infrequency of balloting. But in any event the substantial insulation of voter from agent on matters of public policy is one of the marvels of administrative mischance. Here is a representative, theoretically functioning to carry out his constituents' wishes, waiting nervously for news from back home, for an emergency issue is pending; he seizes upon the newspaper from his home town. But it is an opposition paper. No relief there. The telegraph brings messages, but possibly from persons violently unrepresentative of the majority contemplated in the expression "the greatest good of the greatest number." The baffled agent accordingly has to use his own judgment and vote as he pleases, which, according to Edmund Burke's speech "to the electors at Bristol," is "his jolly good right anyhow." The news from back home is indeed scarcely expected before the next biennial or sextennial election. How democracy can be expected to work out well, how public business can be expected to be transacted in the public interest, when such impassable denseness of medium between official and principal obtains, passes understanding. The informational and instructional facilities for representative government are scarcely different from what would be prescribed for autocracy. It is no great privilege for the voter to have a few chances in his lifetime of voting for persons to hold office if he has no means of saying what he thinks when he thinks it on specific political issues, many of which do not form until after the elected representative has packed his bag after the fall elections. Some attention to the mechanics of communication is recommended for the better functioning of representative government. The voters' pamphlet, issued in several states previous to election, is a promising beginning.

The question arises as to whether the average citizen can be sufficiently interested in public business. He is interested in his private business but tends to be indifferent to public affairs. Part of the time he does not know what is going on and the rest of the time, barring sensational emergencies, he may not care. No such heedlessness attends private business.

Civic lethargy results in part from lack of knowledge, which in turn is related to lack of means of effective communication touching public business. Knowledge breeds interest. The surest way of becoming interested in a subject is to learn something about it. Interest is an emotion of familiarity —familiarity with variations. Civic torpor, the voter's apathy, is due to a large extent to lack of information. The measure of possible civic interest has never yet been taken, for the inadequacy of suitably presented information on public business has precluded.

In this connection let a word be said for public libraries, with men and women of parts in charge. It is high time in the interests of democracy to balance the program of material development with thought materials. Immensely expensive road projects are carried out through regions in which a good public library is nowhere to be found. These same good roads might well be employed to carry books to and from splendid county libraries, especially in the agricultural states. And the librarians should be among the best paid and most carefully selected of public servants.

The deepest root of interest in affairs is that of self-preservation. It requires no urging for the individual to take an interest and see his duty when his welfare is directly and obviously at stake. In private affairs the connection between conditions and welfare is so close that there is no slackening of attention or laxness of circumspection, within the range of the individual intelligence.

Transferred to the wider arena of public business, in which the individual share of responsibility and his share of the returns from social effort are alike less certain and demonstrable, one experiences an immediate loss of motive. The citizen feels that one vote will make little difference, and stays away from the polls. He fails to attend a meeting held for the consideration of a public issue, feeling that his presence is a matter, numerically, of small importance. He stands for graft in city business because he does not see clearly that he is affected or to what extent he is affected. Individuality is lost at the door of public business.

The officeholder is likewise affected with loss of sense of personal significance. He works for the whole public, and a public that may be apathetic and unappreciative. Neither loyalty nor fear is strong as a motive. The sprawling anonymity of public service is a disintegrating influence. Both the citizen and official are under conditions that differ in essential aspects from the motivation of private affairs.

A correction of this psychological deficiency on the part of the voter might be attempted through the larger employment of citizens in consultative capacity, through committees or through the opening of the columns of civic publications for the expression of views and suggestions. Government remains a neglected abstraction as long as the citizen is left with few if any tangible connections with public functions that have their analogue in the colorful bargainings, adventure, initiative and self-assertion of the citizen in his private affairs. It is a well-known fact, that for any coöperative effort to prove successful and appeal to the largest number, there must be diffused participation. Each person must feel that he matters. Every "ladies' aid" knows this, and the woman who sits at the head of a serving table and "pours" is distinctly uplifted. Democratic government, to arouse the emotions that will give it the drive and vigilance needed for permanency and expansion, will have to see to it that a great many people have active participation even in small ways. So far as known, popular government has never made any attempt to base its rule upon the system of motives and interests that, as a matter of fact, do drive in private affairs. By way of illustration, a discovery made in the conduct of successful "parent and teachers' associations" may be cited. It is found that only by participation in meetings of a number of parents and children can these meetings be held up to an active interest. Management and program from the top down do not suffice. The active participation of parents, indeed their investiture with responsibility, and the appearance of their children in an active rôle, are found needful for producing the glow of interest and the devotion comparable to that characteristic of private activity.

Probably such participation in public affairs, a participation beginning on the side of genuine but humble activities, would do more to ensure the permanency of representative and democratic institutions than would any other measure. True, the enlarging of the proportion of the citizen's annual expenditure on the public side and its corresponding diminution in percentage on the private side, would tend to fix his attention on public affairs. If he were to spend less on private employment of a physician and more on the publicly employed physician or state-supported health service, the citizen, thus noting the shifted point of division in his expenditures, would be expected to take a sharper interest in public affairs. If, for sake of argument, John Doe were to spend fifteen hundred dollars for utilities bought privately for private use and another fifteen hundred dollars for utilities bought governmentally for private, but not exclusively private, use, as is the case with all community purchasing, he would follow his dollars as trade follows the flag, or the flag follows trade, as the case may be. Yet in the ultimate psychology of John Doe, the superior effectiveness of motives closely corresponding to those in the private life of wont and custom is unquestionable.

As the case now stands, with but a minor part of expenditure devoted to joint or community utilities, there is small reason to be surprised at the relatively slight amount of citizen interest in public affairs. The citizen does not fully awake to the iniquity of the grafting contractor and the embezzling official. In a city of fifty thousand people, the misuse and waste of a million dollars means only twenty dollars per capita, which is perhaps the price of a ton of coal. This is a small amount in the annual family expenditure, hence a city may be "corrupt and contented." The neighbor's cow in John Doe's sweet-corn patch produces a psychological disturbance vastly more profound. If John Doe were to pursue peccant officials with the same zeal with which he seeks reparation for direct but minor injury, honesty in office would not only be the best policy but the only policy.

Let us say that citizen John Doe spends three thousand dollars a year in living expenses. Of this he spends in taxes a hundred dollars. Twenty-nine hundred dollars go thus in buying things individually and a hundred dollars go in joint purchase of utilities with other citizens. The ratio is 29 to 1. His interest is accordingly about twenty-nine times as great in private affairs as in public. Moreover, he can see and handle the things he gets for the twenty-nine hundred dollars, while the money spent in taxes secures utilities of rather intangible and non-identifiable character. He may buy sanitation with some of the tax money, but who can get enthusiastic about an immunity? He may be thoroughly convinced that what he spends in public purchase is well spent, but he is deprived of the satisfaction of personally planning the purchase and carrying out the transaction and taking home the goods. The intangibility of public purchasing deprives the time-honored art of buying of its dramatic, speculative and concrete elements. Just as the child feels defrauded of an experience when his parents do all the buying and handle the money, so the average man, while assenting to community buying as a necessary practice, nevertheless actually takes more pleasure in buying five dollars' worth of fishing tackle than in joint purchase with a mass of fellow-citizens of a municipal structure costing four million dollars.

Related to the citizen's unimaginative reaction to public expenditure, which is far and away the most economical type of expenditure for net utility, is his singularly atavistic tax psychology. Say "taxes," and the average citizen tends to look downcast. If there is anything a man, economically speaking, ought to be cheerful over it it is economical buying. But does the citizen feel happy over well-spent taxes —over the tax bill? Added to reasons given above touching the psychology of public affairs, there is in the case of taxes—public taxes—the weird phobia that derives from the tea in Boston harbor. There was a time when taxation was identified with tyranny, as in the murderous and unrequited taxing by church and state in France in the heyday of monarchical humbug. When officialdom consisted of a supercargo of licentious tax-eaters, the peasant was justified in gritting his teeth. But now? Don't we want to pay for anything? Should one not rather pay a hundred dollars to the school district than pay a thousand for private tutors? Yet the tax bill throws us into berserker mood. Observe, too, the refined consideration of allowing the other fellow to report more fully his holdings, and the modesty of dodging where possible.

How far the tax emotions are askew may be judged by noting how indifferent the individual is to private taxes—by which is meant the levy of monopoly or profiteering. In a western state an enigmatical rise in the price of coal in one year represented an increase of outlay equaling a sum which would have raised the pay of every school-teacher in that state by several hundred dollars. Was there outcry? As would have been the case if the same sum had been added to the tax bills? Possibly no government could survive like increase in the immediate compensation of its employees. But the added burden in privately contracted debts is followed by no angry reaching for the pillars of the temple. Public expenditure is the first point of attack when the citizen would protect his income.

The reforming of mind on taxation is one of the heavy problems of democratic government in a time when there is a narrowing boundary between anarchy, on the one hand, and intelligent socialization on the other. Can rational attitude and suitable emotion be engendered? When one recalls the objects to which emotion has devotedly attached itself in the years of history, is it too much to hope that with time may come a moral and intellectual readjustment with regard to public effort, public expenditure, community utilities and the economy of making the same amount of money go a longer way? The human mind has immense possibilities of education in wrong directions; why not in the right?

The remaking of mind on the subject of taxation would, however, be a more difficult undertaking than the utilizing of existing attitudes. Observing the comparatively slight objection popularly made to the exaction of profits, one might be inclined to favor raising the immense sums of public expenditure by the profit-taking of public business. Sums that now appear as dividends or profits of privately owned enterprises, especially those like mines and railroads, might thus become available in lieu of direct taxes. The revenue aspect of the tariff illustrates a comparatively painless method of raising public funds. The taxing of excess profits is still another illustration of the slight resistance offered by the consumer to paying taxes indirectly. To subrogate profit-taking public business to monopolistic private business would possibly prove the line of least resistance in the development of taxation policy for the raising of the large sums which assuredly must be raised for public uses.

A needed attitude toward public expenditure may be stimulated by ocular evidence in the form of bargain demonstration, of which an example may be cited. In western states is known the rodent exterminator. Gophers and prairie dogs invade grain fields and wallow and destroy. They eat and destroy millions of bushels of grain. Hence the rodent exterminator. With baits and poisons and knowledge of rodent psychology, the rodent man goes on his way, being paid out of the public taxes. Mathematics being an abstract science, it has been found that statistics have no particular hold on the mind of the member of the board of county commissioners. But the rodents' bodies heaped up in the tonneau of a motor car convince. For giving the eye of faith an eyeful, it has been found by rodent exterminators that nothing does so well as heaping up the bodies of the dead rodents in a car and running such car into the very presence of the county chairman and his board and pointing to the dead gophers and prairie dogs and saying: "Lo, here!" No mental picture of the slaughtered rodents has the persuasive power exercised by the actual physical carcasses, slithering and quaking with motion and drawing the vigilant fly when the engine stops and the crowd gathers. Death is impressive, especially with no process of memory or of imagination intervening. By method the rodent exterminator draws tax warrants in the blood of the slain and evokes his own pay check. He satisfies the taxpayer.

No matter whether one justly prides himself upon the clearness of his images and the definition of his principles or not, he is more firmly convinced and is refreshed in resolution by demonstration. People will not be won to their own welfare unless they see signs. One of the larger activities in popular government must be that of adequate demonstration. Not that every service can be photographed, but at least demonstration can be carried far enough to give the citizen solid ground on which to stand while forming his mind intelligently toward social program and duties.

The citizen's psychology has been explored and exploited by the politician to a nicety; it has been studied minutely. There are practical psychologists at the head in every political campaign. Some of the keenest minds in the country are engaged in political psychology as a means of carrying elections and managing campaigns. Such psychology is of a designing kind in the main, employed not rarely for voting the voters and working the workers. It has no standing with true benevolence and higher statesmanship; it smacks of the smartness of the adroit horse trader with a ringboned nag whose defects he would camouflage; it is not sincere with the fine impersonality of Abraham Lincoln and

Thomas Jefferson; its symbol is the checked vest. Underrate not its technic and achievements. By it the average voter is known better by others than he knows himself.

But of civic psychology in the constructive and idealistic sense how little we know. The citizen has not been analyzed so much with a view to a better state and society. We want not such study of the voter as will perpetuate his deficiencies, but rather enlarge his constructive possibilities and make him a smoothly functioning intelligent unit in the greatest adventure of mankind—self-government. From the known ground of individual and private-life psychology it should be possible to conduct motive and will, habit and conviction, over to skillful and happy coöperation.

In private life the individual finds satisfaction in playing a solo part. Any success that he may thus achieve is unmistakably his own. A fine farm, a handsome residence, a feat of professional performance, a notable business move—all these attach directly to his name. But in many of his relations to the common weal there is no such publicity of success, no such undisguised personality. The employee of the public, serving with others in anonymous coöperation, or the voting citizen, contributing his ballot with thousands or millions of others, has little of the thrill of special attention. To be sure, the prominent public official suffers less from lack of favorable comment and admiration. Indeed he may focus upon himself the glory that logically attaches to helpers and subordinates.

There is compensation for the private in the ranks in the thought that he is one of a distinguished group of workers. But pride in group achievement does not quite fulfill the ambitions of the individual to be known and admired for his efforts. In the motivating of public service, there might well be distinct provisions for appeasing the appetite for individual mention. Indeed, in organization for destruction—war—this principle is recognized by medals and mentions. But the same idea has yet to be recognized suitably for the constructive service rendered by otherwise anonymous men employed by the public for the public. It is all too common a practice in the press and elsewhere to identify a group by the name of its chief, ignoring the thousand and one individuals who severally thirst for having their existence recognized.

The motivation of the prominent official is certain. Men are not wanting to take high office at a sacrifice of income and repose. The reward here is favor in men's eyes. Fame is not only the last infirmity of noble minds but also the first; high office in peace and war attracts irresistibly. It is the motivation of the large number whose services are not particularized and who are usually only casually mentioned by class that presents a critical problem for popular government. To judge by the ordinary textbook in history the Civil War was fought as a series of duels between a handful of stubborn northern generals and a small handful of brilliant southerners. Canals and great public works are also constructed by Herculean individuals practically single-handed.

Some may argue that the fitness or unfitness of the potential voter is measured by the extent to which he takes part in voting. The voter who is so uninformed and apathetic as not to heed election days may be regarded as thus proving that society loses nothing by his absence from the polls. Such interpretation may have a show of correctness, but it can scarcely be thought a good omen for democratic government when there is indifference to the ballot. It would be a more favorable condition if every person, man and woman, entitled to vote, were to become so conscious of the franchise as to make neglect impossible.

In this connection the possibility of finding a stimulus in publicity suggests itself. Suppose every precinct established a public roll of eligible voters, and that at the close of election day every name were crossed off except those of persons failing to vote. It is quite likely that such bad eminence of the neglectful would speedily bring out the laggards. Once thus brought to the habit of voting, there would very likely ensue a pronounced growth of intelligent interest in elections on the part of those who have lacked vision. And, on the part of educated but cynical citizens, there would be a tendency to attack those obstacles and perversions which have too often made the cultivated wash their hands of politics.

Assurance that public business can be motivated, both on the part of the voter and on that of the public employee, is afforded by the fact that big business is a reality with no convincing signs of early collapse. In big business are the phenomena of subordination, anonymity, diffused participation, remoteness of final output and intangibility of individual contribution. Yet big business thrives. Its problems are not so difficult as those of big public business. Its methods are unquestionably more psychological, especially in the past few years.

Bonuses, promotions, personal mention, pensions, emulation, the personal touch, welfare, "mothering," and what not are brought into play to steady the bees as they collect the honey. These methods are an innovation in business, it is true, and obtain most in enterprises that are most advanced and freest from the older industrial traditions. But they serve as points of brilliant contrast to conditions in public service. Not until the welfare of the employee is as much esteemed in public as in private business will the psychological foundations of democracy be made secure. After all, no government that does not place the happiness of the individual above that of a mythical state consisting of no individuals in particular, deserves to prosper or to be served with enthusiasm. The wheels of government might well stop; they have no business not to stop, until, say, the future of a worn-out worker in a department of public service is assured. Such ideas as that a faithful public employee may be turned out summarily, or that one must expect to sacrifice if he is to work for others through the mechanism of state coöperation, naturally result in inferior quality in public institutions.

The control of the voter over government implies to a degree the control of the layman over the professional, the control of the unskilled over the skilled. Government increasingly tends toward specialization and expertness. The expansion of political government over the industrial and economic field carries further the principle of division of labor and technical efficiency. Apart from major policies it is difficult for the voter to instruct governmental functionaries. Recognizing the point to which we have arrived, some would say let experts govern and let there be a short and infrequent ballot.

The relation of the voter to the expert in functions of government is like that of layman to the specialist privately employed. Without taking the case out of the physician's hands, the patient exercises authority. He does so at a risk, it is true. The relations of the architect to his employer are readily established with due regard to expert knowledge and directive preferences. The citizen, like the layman employing a professional, has the advantage of a general view. The architect, the landscape engineer, the bacteriologist, the insurance man and the nasal specialist are all specialized to purpose rather than for balance. The voter is a kind of specialist in judging how things look to a layman. The human race would not be the same again if no longer might one venture an opinion rather beyond his knowledge.

The dominating aim of public business is to secure more widely diffused benefits than are hoped for under the restricted and incidental philanthropy of private enterprise. Easier access to necessities and utilities is sought through socialized agencies. This aim can be realized only by skillful employment of human factors. The success of public enterprise cannot be assured in defiance of the nature of the individual whose abilities must be enlisted. An atmosphere of freedom, rewards for high ability, quick returns for daring and resourcefulness, prizes to initiative and skill—all these considerations must be heeded in the interests of successful group enterprise; at any rate these must be heeded as much as in private enterprises. It is not to be overlooked that private enterprise has evidently come far short of perfection; it has failed to heed the larger relationships—has been local, provincial, selfish and non-social in spirit; its shortcomings have given rise to the powerful tendency toward the extension of governmental function as a possibly superior means of welfare.

PART II

THE SOCIAL MIND AT CLOSER RANGE

IX

INSTINCTIVE TENDENCY AS AFFECTING SOCIAL CONDITIONS

Civilization through planning is yet to be developed; vision and coördinated effort for social well-being are less in evidence than are muddling through in response to instinctive tendency. The planning for careers on the part of individuals is not paralleled by similar foresight on the part of social and governmental management. Trial and error methods and reliance upon naïve predilection play a larger part in social procedure than in well-ordered private lives. Due to the neglect of training for citizenship, thinking socially is not so far advanced as thinking professionally and commercially. Courts for settling private differences appeared long before attempts at international organization, and the duel passed long before the idea of salving national honor rationally made its appearance. Nations and social groups rely on special providence, turns of luck, and cure without a doctor, much more than does the citizen in his private affairs.

The ways of meeting problems may be arranged in serial order. The lowest form of response is that of random, and profuse and blindly instinctive conduct. Thus, a rat in a cage will rush madly about, bumping against all parts of the cage indiscriminately, with some chance of escape through striking a loose wire, calculation playing no part.

To invoke the aid of memory represents a higher type of effort for escaping dangers and securing benefits. Thus, to find solution through recall of what oneself or others have done before in similar situations is a distinct advance over the method of frenzy and exhaustion.

But the highest kind of procedure is to analyze the problem, conceive of alternatives, test the alternatives mentally and select the most auspicious. The reasoning method is highly economical and more satisfactory in the face of novel difficulties. Not that this method is invariably used apart from the lower methods, for the more primitive responses contribute something to the composite process. When draymen attempt to carry a couch through a narrow passageway all of these methods are liable to be represented. One helper may try the rat psychology of main strength and chance success; another may recall an experience with a similarly refractory piece of furniture; while another of the trio analyzes the stairway and visualizes a safe exit. The prosperity of the couch and stairway lies here with the visualizer.

The greatest of social needs is that for the visionary, the thinker, the idealist. He may consider alternatives that are not practicable; but the function of holding up possibilities of social program is of vital importance. And yet how society, weltering in instinct, shuns the innovator and the theorist. The entomologist is a "bugologist," the anatomist and physician a "sawbones," the scholar a "bookworm," the sociologist a "red."

Yet society is in more danger from excessive expression of instinct than from philosophies. A far greater rationalization is necessary to insure social stability and develop organization and system. The function of speculation and theorizing, of proposing remedies and posing queries, of challenging tradition and reviewing customs, is an invaluable one. It is the demonstrated means of advancement in industrial and scientific fields, and is no less fitting and prolific in social program. Social scepticism and active research represent the higher form of intelligence as contrasted with instinct with its ineffectual twitchings of remedy or its frantic and costly tragedies of war and revolution. Without vision the people perish. The age of good politics and happy economics must be an age of reason, with the Merlins left isolated with their curses. The harrying of the intellectual represents disregard and waste of social resources to which proud recognition should be given. With the ban on free and accusatory intelligence, with dogma protected by officers and mobs, society risks progressive deterioration. Evil forces in modern society are those that stand against incisive and untrammeled political and economic utterance; they represent the viewpoint of the heresy hunters and hounders of scientists in the centuries when intellectual and religious life was at low ebb. That the dogging of the intellectual appeals to classes of lowest culture level makes the business uniquely impertinent. Until learning, in all fields, and the exercise of the rational faculties are exalted as social righteousness, we invite the fate that awaits vital ignorance.

Reliance upon intellectual means and forces rather than upon the impulsions of mere instinct suggests itself as eminently desirable for the adjustment of industrial problems. Industrial war reveals at every point the dominance of an unevolved system of ideas and motivation.

The strike is a notable example of an instinctive rather than a rational attempt to correct evils. In strategy for immediate results and minor ameliorations, the strike perhaps has occasional value. But as a social method it corresponds to the tactics of a rat seeking its escape violently from a trap the nature of which is not perceived. The petty revolution of the trade strike, the larger revolution of the general strike, and the major revolution of the social overthrow, besides leaving matters much as they were before, give unwholesome persistence to inept method. They signify an incapacity or lassitude in the exercise of the rational powers, which are preëminently the powers upon which ordered welfare must rely. Strikes and wars are not constructive; they cannot be lastingly constructive because they are expedients of force in place of justice. True, the technic of war and revolution and strikes may be rationalized, but the rationalizing falls short of social synthesis; these phenomena are the phenomena of primitive reaction, and there is no health in them. One tenth of the money lost to wages in strikes of the past twenty-five years would have provided the workers with culture agencies out of which might have come a rational procedure commending itself generally. The principal disadvantage of the workers is ignorance, and strikes do little to obviate this. Lasting benefits can come only with enlightenment and specific understanding. Happily labor colleges are appearing, and the employment of statisticians and advisers promises the transfer of labor problems to the arena of scientific and rational adjustment. It would doubtless, in the long run, be a blessing to labor if strikes were banned. Modern nations have hit upon the ballot as a means of securing general welfare and of liquidating the just grievances of groups. It is for labor to qualify for intelligent use of this same instrument. The instinctive and juvenile disposition to smash things and to trust in the good luck of spontaneous readjustment is distinctly out of place in a time calling for calculation. The ideal of labor should be that of rational rather than essentially instinctive method.

Equipped with natural tendencies which took shape under the simpler conditions of precivilization, mankind ever tends to recapitulate its past when faced by newer conditions. Just as a dog may try to bury a bone on a hardwood floor or attempt to hide its milk-dish by pawing dirt into it—recapitulating primitive canine history under inappropriate circumstances—so all of us, reeking with the primitive, are prone to inconvenient atavisms in the new circumstances of the world. An example is tribal psychology in politics, reminiscent of the effectual unification of the primitive group.

Though the major parties in England and the United States are indistinguishable in principle and practice, yet the thrall of party names and of party leaders is potent. Allegiance is given willingly, nay, enthusiastically, to candidates and as forcefully withheld from other candidates not because of significant differences, but from influence of tribal deities, totem poles, war cries, paint and feathers. The tribe itself, apart from leaders and major beneficiaries, does not well perceive that unity in diversity which so often prevails beneath insignia. The true clansman goes with the plaid. The sense of familiarity of symbols satisfies. What the verities are does not always matter. It was only yesterday that the independent voter made his appearance under the derisive epithet of "Mugwump." It was nothing short of scandalous when citizens charily ventured to follow principles rather than the time-honored chieftain. The office-seeker, however, was less victimized by party. Party fealty to him oftentimes meant something else; it was the promise of things to come.

Through unwarranted survival of tribalism, the citizen is blinded and civically nonconstructive. The decline of instinctive partisanship is therefore auspicious, for the voter thus becomes mobile and free to judge for himself. Attention turns to measures and mere chieftainship diminishes in prestige. The sublimation of personal loyalty appears in devotion to causes and principles, and the utilizing of leaders or parties without being submerged in these. Organizations become convenient instrumentalities, without fixedness of individual within party regardless of realities of principle and character. The tendency for citizens to migrate from one party to another needs only to become associated with cause to be truly promising. Migration for a change of luck is not fully satisfying. Rational migration will doubtless increase, but migration from any motive is better than irrevocable status.

Arrest of development on the plane of clansmanship means indifference to the larger group and too exclusive attachment to party, sect, county (as in the South), college, city, or state. The modern community is as wide as humanity, and the program of civilization involves the passing away of the provincial point of view. The emotional states propagated by small organizations may oppose consciousness of the wide community. Secret societies, churches, and social sets that confirm in any way their memberships in emotional provincialisms thus render a social dis-service. A positive culture of catholicity is implied by the closer relations of commerce and world communication. The ideal of social oneness, which the family, the village and the sect and party have stressed within narrow limits, can be made to cover this minor planet, whose circumference has been registered on the milometers of millions of automobiles.

There is a possibility that nationalistic patriotism may remain an emotional fact long after the reality supporting it becomes a skeleton. National self-sufficiency has largely passed away. What nation is not now virtually a state in an internation? Foreign wealth may finance the railroad on which one rides; capital is internationalized; foreign-owned capital is rooted wherever one turns—in farm loans, public utility plants, railroads, packing houses, insurance businesses. Foreign elements of population swarm about us. No conquered country could be inundated by aliens more completely than has happened in time of peace. Masses of people have gone from state to state in the internation in time of peace.

Such mobility of world population will continue. Legislation in recognition of different standards of living and for birth control may affect amount, but not, in the long run, the fact of migration. The laws of mating, which little heed nationality, are pitted against inelastic nationalism. We shall have to adjust our minds to the present facts of internationalism and make ready for world legislation and federation. Our emotional and intellectual preparation for community life on the planet is backward.

Whereas the sense of provincialism was an outgrowth from tribal and geographical restrictions, the spirit of adventuring operated to give primitive man a certain variety of experience. Early man led a life of adventure, ranging for food along the river beds and by the sea, where he was constantly meeting the unexpected. The stamp of vicissitude is in our nervous systems, and when life does not present us with sufficient excitement we go in search of it. Necessity, in terms of strange beasts, peering enemies and food shortage, gave a turn to consciousness in primitive life which cannot be satisfied in man to-day without resort to occasional adventure. Penned in by the apartment house and modern conveniences, man to-day takes his adventuring symbolically and by proxy to a large extent. He fights by reading of pugilistic encounters, swims by mentally following Leander across the Hellespont, skulks through the spooky darkness of night with the hero of a detective story, finds thrills in the "movies," and invests his money in wildcat stocks.

Indeed the expression of the instinct of adventure through speculation and investment is an outstanding fact and socially a significant fact. It is not too much to claim that the character of industrial and economic life is intimately related to the adventure instinct, and that proposed social reform which does not adequately recognize this fact is doomed to miscarry. It might seem that the presence of the wage system is evidence that the adventure instinct has become atrophied. Fixedness of income by wages does not appeal to the venturesome, it is true. The wagering impulse, which is a form of the instinct of adventure, is a motive which plays an important rôle in so-called independent businesses, like farming and the retail store.

The wage-earner, however, is not without recourse. He may adventure with his savings, and it is a commonplace of observation that one may have as much fun with a venturesome 25-cent piece as with sizable sums. The strangely placid and much bedamned bourgeoisie, the immovable obstacle to reform by revolution, obtain their adventure by investment, rather than attempt it by the more spectacular methods of the expropriated. Society is above all else a psychological organism, true to the original instincts shaped and supported in primitive, natural conditions. The sense of adventure is not lacking in the class of small owners; it insists on finding satisfaction. The adventure may appear illusory, but as long as the illusion holds—it holds.

The small-business man and the farmer and the person of the middle class who has some capital, however small, invested in business or in stocks is an adventurer. He hopes, often against reasonable hope, for wealth. There is excitement in pursuit. The lucky turn of stocks, the "bumper" crop, the imagined run of brisk sales—these constitute a satisfying program of economic adventure. Capitalism can never be shaken as long as bonds and securities are widely held by the middle and lower economic classes. The Wall Street magnate is not more emotionally compromised by the spirit of speculation—not more sentimentally attached to economic individualism—than is the clerk who buys a share of stock at 35 and watches the quotations to follow its ascent above par. The dividends on widely held shares of the profiteering joint-stock companies of ancient Rome served as hush money to the voters, while the orgy of exploitation was undermining the empire.[1]

The instinct of adventure, expressed as a wagering interest in employment of means, not only determines the character of the concepts and terms of business, but exposes the people to enormously costly and consequential raids upon small capitals, with no slight results toward abnormal and society-wrecking centralization of wealth. The readiness of the average man of small means to take a chance in investment, to believe in the "pot of gold at the foot of the rainbow," to send out his savings on perilous adventure, especially to fall under the enchantment of distance when investing, is the strong foundation of the "gold-brick" industry. The earning of money is but a part of the process of securing individual and social welfare. The spirit and conditions of investment are fully as important.

The petty investor who happens to be humbugged

---

1 Abbott, *The Common People of Ancient Rome*. Chapter on Corporations.

and plucked through the bait of hope of sudden wealth not only loses economically—in the aggregate such losses are of critical magnitude—but he also exemplifies and perpetuates a functioning of an instinct of singular weakness and ill omen. "Blue sky" laws recognize, if they do not cure, the malady. Social cohesion is hardly possible to economic ends when there is individual confidence in miraculous salvation and special providences of speculation. The wagering elements of the farmer's occupation have kept him full of faith, with the result that coöperation gains little foothold in the farming class. Among millions of people faith in a transforming luck and adventure makes the individual as resistant to social and economic amalgamation as a particle of zero snow is unsuited to form part of a snowball. Consciousness of a common cause and of a common lot is excluded by the disposition to bet on one's own luck. Just as monarchy is upheld by a group, each of whom counts on special favors, so top-heavy plutocracy is upheld by the non-coöperation of the many who individually hope for great rewards, apart from the calculable returns of patient labor. It is even an axiom among promoters of shady speculative ventures that every man is willing to be victimized at least once.

Scars of purse, like wounds of battle, are presumptive evidence of valor.

The psychology of the "gold brick" mind is related to adventure, but it goes beyond that. It has been a fallacy of thought in America to assume that everybody is not only, by the Declaration of Independence asserted to be created equal, but that in individual consciousness everybody feels equal. Nothing could be further from the truth than the feeling of equality. The gregariousness which marks man as well as animals of lower organization implies a readiness to follow leaders and to submerge one's own personality. Within limits, abuse of authority is expected and admired. Little resentment attaches to high-handed treatment by superior individuals. Persons having the attributes of leadership are strangely indulged by the multitude. A liar and swindler who is smooth, who shows pedigree, may be voted charming rather than otherwise. The percentage of people who inherit a full code of self-respect or arrive at it by experience and reflection is small indeed. There are great blocks of people in democracies as well as in monarchies whose outstanding characteristic is embryonic self-respect and primitive servility. Mobility of modern societies has displaced the more abject prostrations, but individual assertion is habitually deflated in an endless number of cases—a fact that shows in the unreflective adoption of fashions, editorial views, propagandas, and in mute long-suffering. Millions of people have regarded a living wage as an ideal for themselves, without going so far as to claim an economically safe old age. They have been contented with little—abject. The strength of the king has lain in the craving of the common man to have a foot on his neck.

Now it is just as much to the advantage of the classes as to the masses to have a widely diffused self-respect. Industry needs the stimulus which comes from a market insistent upon plentiful and excellent production. No manufacturer likes to turn out rubbish, and no dealer likes to sell it over the counter or from his warehouses. The more wants the people develop and the more exacting and refined their demands, the higher are the possibilities of trade and wealth production. Civilization implies an increase and refinement of wants. The man who is contented with little and that of poor quality is the original enemy of industry. The worker who is satisfied with a living wage is not so good a citizen, nor in the long run so good an employee, as one who wants a saving wage. The ultimate consuming power, and therefore market demand, is increased by the larger assertion of economic interest. If one manufacturer employed workers who insisted upon a saving wage while his competitor was able to secure employees satisfied with a living wage, the former proprietor would be at a disadvantage. But if workers claimed a saving wage the net results would include larger support for taxation, less expense for charity, less sickness, and national economy.

Production is in its infancy; the recession of servile attitude is a prerequisite for its highest development. A needed stimulus is withheld if the public puts up with literature of a kind that makes the novel writer blush, accepts without complaint less than the best that art can supply, or eats poor food without felt humiliation. The cult of lowly cheerfulness and sunbeam compliance does what it can to start society on the downward path. The ability of the meek and lowly to do harm incidentally is perhaps equaled by that of no other class.

X

CONSTRUCTIVE EXPRESSION OF MOTIVES

The deep-seated tendencies with which we are born, and which insistently demand outlet, are capable of finding expression in a variety of forms. The specialization of instinct in man is not pronounced. Even children, in whom instinct is least overlaid with conventional habit, show slight tendency to react with the uncanny perfection of inherited movement exhibited by chickens, puppies, kittens and birds. Human instincts function as large patterns of tendency, the ultimate character of which is effectually established by training, example, suggestion, and culture. Man has been said to have more instincts than any other animal. But his instincts are the most faded, the most plastic, the most transformed.

The nervous and bodily mechanism seeks activity, for there is a reservoir of energy which thrusts the child forward into contacts and experimentation with resistless power. The little world of home is explored on its physical side. Objects are tested by the organs of sensation. Later the muscular endowment seeks gratification in the doing of things. There is ceaseless activity, at first of ill-coördinated character and vague purpose, but increasingly purposeful and skilled.

This original tendency to physical activity ultimately is harnessed to vocations and subjected to repression and direction. The forms of the individual's physical expression, his motor and bodily repertory, come to assume a definite set. Oftentimes this ultimate range of physical expression is inadequate in the light of personal and social possibilities.

The happy abandon of the child's expression of physical interests is rarely equalled in the adult stage. It is unquestionable that modern life loses immeasurably through the hardening of the physical activities to gainful pursuits and the muscular reticence of leisure. Full, free physical existence, which is the very mandate of the instinct of physical activity, encounters social barriers, from the bondage of conventional clothing to abstention from the many diverting things that a person might do if he could forget his dignity. There is much yet to be achieved in revising the list of what a grown person may do without shocking the neighbors. Neither the laborer, who becomes a veritable cart horse for mechanical fixation of movements and immobility of muscle groups, nor the person who "enjoys" a life in ruts of respectable restraint can be cited as an example of the ideal physical being.

In a large number of cases the individual's life is unbalanced as between physical and mental expression, and in many cases boredom, irritability, a sense of futility, mental stagnation, or vicious tendencies spring directly out of physical restraint and lack of motor program. The ultimate social effects of a better distribution and a better selection of ways of employing the physical powers would be transforming. This wider use of the human physical equipment could be effected through revision and extension of vocational opportunities, and especially through universal provision for avocations having stimulating physical factors. It is a fact quite uncomplimentary to civilization that there are so many who so often do not know what to do with themselves—so many who do not know how much more varied their physical experiences might become. Modern life is a pent-up life. It presents plenty of examples of excessive physical strain but fewer or a rationalized physical program, rich, varied and joyfully responding to the range of natural opportunities.

Mentally there are likewise many who do not know what to do with themselves. The original tendency to mental activity is not sufficiently specific to guarantee intellectual prosperity in the adult. Direction, encouragement, reward, and freedom are essential. With all the culture materials that the world has accumulated, there is yet lack of available culture materials for millions of people. What to read, what to study, how to investigate—these are matters that cannot well be left to chance. The best natural mind is almost helpless under privations of culture. The supplying of significant culture materials for all is an important function in society. There are great gaps of illiteracy and still greater gaps of not knowing what to read when literate. A commercial pandering and timid educational effort—unambitious and time-serving rather than exultingly dominant educational effort—are ingloriously acquiesced in. Every person is potentially an intellectual in the literal and undisputed sense of the word. Trivial, misguided, and blind-alley uses of mind are not inevitable. The factor of intelligence is slowly, too slowly, approximating its proper standing as an ideal and a practical utility.

The problem of securing fuller and finer social expression of the impulses to physical and mental activity is one that may be attacked as a problem of faulty distribution of wealth. But, to judge by the effects of wealth upon the individual under conditions as they now exist, the rationalizing of distribution would not necessarily carry with it a knowledge of the best use of life. How to live is a problem that has yet to be solved and resolved. It is a question that has been answered with dogma and clouded with sentimentalism. It can scarcely be maintained that satisfactory progress has been made in laying out the procedure for the best possible life. Millions of people, doubtless, learn late in life things that would have increased their happiness greatly, if known long before. In a sense, all knowledge and science are a basis for the best life. But a more conscious attempt to find the best employments of physical and mental energies would not be incompatible in an age which attempts to find the best in minor and relative things. For want of another word the term *eubiology* may be proposed to signify the art that would give society less the aspect of the pursuit of happiness than of its attainment.

For the achievement of the best possible life, resources are available of which, possibly, too little use is made. The lives of men and women of experience abound in materials of much significance. These materials are often less accessible for popular guidance than is desirable. It is doubtful if any information imparted to the young through the usual courses of study could compare favorably with the instruction that might be gleaned from their elders of widest and best experience. The failure to draw upon such sources more fully reveals inadequacy of method rather than challenges the value of the kind of knowledge mentioned. The net result of failure to utilize more fully the riches of ripe experience is to retard the development of the young and contribute to social confusion.

The annexation of others' experience through processes of learning implies special activities of the instinct of curiosity. Scientist, economic student, social interpreter, historian, and business analyst represent the turn that instinctive curiosity may take. Curiosity, which serves as feelers of the mind, has had a checkered career as a reputable instinct. Instead of being hopefully stimulated curiosity has, not infrequently, come in for family spankings and social disapproval. Lacking proper outlet and ventilation, curiosity, the itch for knowledge, may turn to the local and the trivial.

Such progress as has not been accidental has preceded from curiosity, the inquisitive turn of mind lifted to the higher levels of consciousness. Hence it is unfortunate when curiosity is dampened, as dampened it may be by parental taboo and social purblindness. The arrest of this tendency on the plane of the poolroom and the sewing club is a social misfortune. Cultural direction of curiosity, its fostering for developments in industry, in the professions and in social achievements, has great possibilities.

Emphasis upon the amassing of information rather than upon procedure has the effect of dulling the searching instinct. The feeling that everything has been found out that can be found out, that all that is left to do is to learn what some one else has discovered, is an unpromising state of mind. The physician does not usually ask how much the patient has in his stomach but what his appetite is. The telling fact about the supposedly educated person is not his erudition, but his alertness. The number and muscularity of the questions one proliferates, their relevancy and incisiveness, is a better indication of a going mind than the memory mass of facts. Even in the professions of expert service where knowledge counts critically, it is reassuring to encounter the type of intelligence that forever plays over information, is forever scanning and curious. One cannot know what facts mean without knowing facts, but one may know facts and not know what they mean. It would be a fair test, if an unconventional one, for schools to graduate only upon the showing of evidence that the candidate has a mind full of inquiry, of problems he might hope to solve, of places he would like to visit, of books he looks forward to reading, of impressions he would like to verify, of propositions he would like to test, of personages he would like to interview; who would, in short, continue to learn.

The instinct of curiosity is genetically interwoven with the activities by which early man obtained his living. The hunting and fishing and finding stage preceded agriculture. The games of children are notably a pantomime of hunting. There is a wild primitive joy in running down game symbolically. Finding hidden articles and playing tag as well as the overt chase of small animals reveal the inheritance of the impulse that lies anciently back of the bow and arrow, the weapons of bronze and stone, and the stealthy stalking of game. Primitive man, if not eating regularly three times a day, ate no doubt a quantitative equivalent, and if he missed his aim he went hungry. Hunting and dietary were as right and left hands.

Instincts are known not only by their unabashed appearance in the simple minds of children but as well in the preferred diversions of the grown-ups. Hunting and fishing make their universal appeal. These pursuits indeed simulate "pure" science and the fine arts in putative aloofness from the money interest. For since about 1850 it is likely that every pound of fish taken in the lesser bodies of water by the angler has cost far more than it was worth, financially speaking—perhaps on the average twenty-five dollars a pound. For economic returns amateur fishing and hunting have long since passed over to pursuits not vitiated by commercialism. They testify to the downright delight of giving the cave man his innings. Moreover, when there is good luck, does the angler stop casting or the sportsman cease firing? Not so. He then fishes and hunts for the whole tribe—only the game laws stop him, and then not if he can help it. A peculiarity of instinct is, that it never knows when to quit—presenting alike the danger of overdoing, and the zest that animates persistent activity.

Modern conditions deny primitive form of expression to the hunting instinct, which more and more has diminished to recreation and stimulating outings. But the original tendency persists and finds sublimated expression in many fields, in efforts to secure employment and maintenance. It is indeed one of the principal motivations that modern life has derived from the original nature of man. We use the vocabulary of hunting and fishing. We "hunt" for lost articles and "fish" for compliments. A man "hunts" a job. People make "killing" remarks.

The hunting interest has motivated biological work and studies in natural history. Darwin hunted until he became shocked at the sight of a bird he had wounded, and thereafter refrained from gun hunting. His *Voyage of the Beagle* is, however, a beautiful example of scientific hunting. The intentness, circumspection, perseverance and interest in wild nature that are identified with primitive hunting, are outstanding traits of his researches. Theodore Roosevelt united the original hunting interest with its sublimated expression in natural history, the latter dominating; he explained his willingness to shoot to kill on the ground that wild animals usually meet death by violence anyhow. The study of birds and their hunting with the camera take the place of destructive hunting, and there is the bag of names and particulars in place of actual trophies of capture.

There is no end to the supplementary and symbolical forms of expression of the hunting tendency. Conceived in terms of search and hunt, all sorts of social objectives make appeal. Some of the early Judean fishermen became fishers of men and made their nets thereafter of words and example. The physician may resent a suggestion as to the cause of the patient's complaint, preferring rather to hunt for it himself; besides, his marksmanship is not to be impugned. Let the garageman find out the trouble himself; he likes to hunt. Ask a man to do a particular thing and he may feel tired; ask him to help with his superior hunting ability and he will leave his dinner.

The hunting interest, in its varied phases of search, pursuit, outwitting, and capture, may be used to social ends in problems of poverty, underconsumption, unemployment and disease. Perhaps the money hunt takes precedence to-day; it need not be so indefinitely. It does not dominate over this interest in the case of the explorer and the inventor. To hunt constructively for the common good fulfills the terms of the chase similarly with the hunt merely for the acquisition of personal fortune.

The fighting tendency, the disposition to repel dangers by force, is a reaction called forth by the challenge of harm from any source. Under primitive conditions harm came often with animals and strangers, hence fighting was with weapons and in a physical setting. With civilization the dangers that beset are less and less immediately physical ones, and more and more of a kind involving for defense a mobilization of intelligence and the use of the intangible forces of argument and ideas.

Conflict is transferred to the arena of the press, the platform, and the polls. The efficient fighter is one who prevails with the weapons with which issues are ultimately settled, and issues are not settled by force—physical force applied to a thought relation is like the use of a hammer in place of a telescope. Modern heroes of combat are found in the political arena and in civic enterprise, and are engaged in overcoming prejudice and championing reforms. Combats are waged about propositions that have a physical reference, as waterways, railroads, foreign-made goods, sites of public buildings and the like, but the instrumentalities of combat are mental and without physical body. They are ideas, used for persuasion, surprise, conviction, exhaustion. Force of utterance and vigor of language propel ideas; but it is not often, except in the catastrophic reversion and panic of war and the abrogation of intelligence represented by tar and feathers, that force is anything but symbolic. The irritated legislator may rush down the aisle and collar his adversary, but the headlines show that other members of the august body immediately intervened before physical harm was done. It is indeed impressive to observe a man of large physique forcefully expounding his views with belligerent gesture, strong and provocative voice, attitude of attack and mimic violence, no adversary being present—the occasion being simply a public meeting for discussion of a gas franchise. Combat has been raised to a higher than physical plane, though the ancient mechanics of combat survive in gesture, intonation, pose of facing the enemy and mimic pounding with closed fist and biting with glistening oratorical teeth.

Let no one think that occasions for fighting, symbolically, have diminished with decrease of actual physical encounter. Life is a battle in more senses now than in the simpler ages when famine and ignorance kept down the population. More issues and more complex ones develop with us than appeared in earlier times, and general increase of intelligence has multiplied critics and potential competitors. Now, as in seemingly more heroic times, courage and will prevail, though measures instead of men invoke the combative spirit.

The protective and assertive quality of pugnacity, so often associated with destructive conflict, has possibilities for constructive enterprise. Peace has its victories no less than war; but the contests for creative achievement involve to the full the hardihood of the fighting spirit. The material and social obstacles to higher general welfare afford an ample field for exercise of the energies that formerly were associated with the doughty warrior and the quarrelsome member of the tribe. There is never a time when there is not a fight of some description—indeed many fights—for social objectives; and there is scarcely a desirable attainment, individual or social, that is not a challenge to fortitude.

Primitive contest for mates, food and advantage is echoed in mind to-day in the spirit of rivalry and emulation. The rivalry tendency thrusts itself forward as a sense of competition. This tendency is one of the most uncomfortable that we possess. It serves the purpose of stimulating to needed activities, but it also keeps us awake at night with recollections of tactical mistakes and apprehensions of competitors' coups. As far as comfort is concerned the instinct of rivalry might better be in the Red Sea.

What escape is there from the raw force and pattern of jealousy, envy, rivalry, disparagement, competition, dispraise? Can society ever be welded together without fatal flaws unless this tendency be restrained and modified? The unmodified, unsublimated instinct is capable of misleading to bickerings and social disharmony and inadequacy. It is the foe to coöperation. Families, communities, schools, committees, go on the rocks through personal rivalry.

One thing that keeps rivalry going is the fear that some one else will not play fair, that he may take undue advantage. Absolute fair play assuages rivalry. Instead of trusting others as presumable friends, we watch them as enemies, and they reciprocate. If one had the courage to believe nothing but good of people, nations included, what would happen? Should we be eaten up? It is unlikely. The result would rather be that our example would be imitated.

The socially dissolving and acidlike quality of detraction suggests a treatment that Liberty Hyde Bailey proposes for dandelions in the lawn; he says, "admire them and leave them there." Blindly instinctive emulation and conceit take in too much territory. The victim of self-love and sensitive vanity joins issue with too many competitors and for too many comparisons. In a day of specialization it cannot be expected that any one person can assert equivalents of merit and achievement with a whole group. Individuals are not sufficiently comparable to make it advisable to institute personal comparison on a large scale. Whole-hearted recognition of the valuable qualities of other individuals and other races is a social cement. Indiscriminate praise or denunciation of a people, as the Jews, the Mexicans, or the English, is directly opposed to good sense and veracity; it provokes animosity rather than helps to establish a synthetic and catholic view of the many, though not necessarily identical, excellencies of different types of culture.

Coöperation is impossible as long as attention is fixed on differences. Only by focusing on common purpose and cultivating admirations without rivalry can coöperative enterprise be successfully carried forward, be it a public school in a community of Lutherans and Catholics, Swedes and Poles—or Canadian and American coöperation to keep the three thousand miles of boundary free from cannon.

The political or industrial manipulator sows discord by dragging into the focus of attention the inevitable differences which exist in any group. Press the button of religious differences and economic coöperation flies out of the window; harp on differences rather than recognize merits, and no two nations, even English-speaking nations, could live in peace. The technic of harmony calls for elimination of reference to differences, and emphasis upon common interests. The world has made a great advance in method since the days when pamphleteers hurled abusive epithets at one another and political rivals exploited their opponents' personal shortcomings. What discussion has lost in coarse picturesqueness it has gained in auspicious reticence.

The instinct of personal decoration and display shows in children and governs the dress of savages, who subordinate utility to ornament. Ornamentation of self is closely related to mating and to social survival; for display not only actually attracts the eye, but implies the possession of physical or mental qualities of practical value. The savage who adorns himself with bear and elk-tooth necklaces exhibits evidence of his prowess as a hunter; his trophies are his credentials. Jewelry performs a like function to-day as evidence of success in the money hunt, the compacting of values in small space being neatly accomplished by diamond studs and pearl earrings.

Display may take many forms. Foreign words and phrases are sometimes employed for show. Some studies, said Francis Bacon, are for ornament. Latin has been affected for the purpose, and even more so, French. Titles are de luxe forms of social display. Secret societies manufacture honorific titles and distinctions which insure the possession by members of verbal, typographical, or costume prominence. It would be a denial of life itself to challenge the function of display; but the preferred forms of display measure and project social ideals. There has been progress beyond muscular and surface physical display. Increasingly clothing has taken on utility and departed from the merely ornamental. The stage and the stagelike social occasion, the holiday and the infrequent festivity, preserve the traditions of ornateness of apparel; but science and utility turn ancient pomps to a kind of levity. The acrobat and pugilist, as representatives of a physical claim to social approval, appeal less forcefully to-day than did similar performers in the days of the serious splendors of tournament and court.

The shift from physical decoration to ornaments of mind and character marks a considerable progress. This transfer of emphasis has been less pronounced in the case of woman, who must overcome the economic resistance to marriage, and, when married, often functions as an economic barometer. But the tendency among women to supplement physical with other elements of display is unmistakable. The plainly dressed woman in science or business is not a rarity. Some claim to attention is imperative, and the individual apparently neglectful of outward appearance invariably has his preferred forms of display, which may even produce weightier results for contrasting with neglect of dress and equipage. Apparently to flout customary forms of impressing observers is to imply resources out of the ordinary. The well-known and well-established may therefore safely spurn the latest cut and the newest model.

In reciprocity of admiration and display lies a possibility of raising to effective strength ideals that signify much for a better state of society—concepts of what fame and approval should attach to reveal the inwardness of popular mind. It is notorious that the quiet, constructive careers of the pioneer who makes a beautiful farm out of the wilderness and of the self-effacing woman who is the good angel of a community are less blazoned than the success of the man who simply gets rich. The useful person who does not advertise himself can be rescued from oblivion by an alert appreciation by others. The idea back of the Carnegie hero fund has the advantage of shifting to the community the detection of merit and its publicity; it is a foreshadowing of a type of admiration not vitiated by the design or vanity of the recipient. The kinds of display that have historically won popular admiration do not necessarily meet the demands of the present. There is nothing that calls for nicer discrimination than what to applaud, and nothing that is likely to do more to shape the trend of institutions.

Like other instincts, fear is a general tendency whose ultimate forms of expression are governed largely by experience and training. This is not to say that certain situations do not naturally evoke fear, for such is the case. High places, wild animals, strange faces, the dark bodies of water, the forest, snakes, thunder and lightning, and the dead, have exceptional power to arouse fears. There is a gentle current of fear at almost all times, a current that is readily expanded to anxiety, dread or terror.

This susceptibility has in past ages received abhorrent culture, being played upon by design for the control of men. Savages stand in awe of evil spirits and are tied hand and foot by fearsome taboos. The early Greeks, rationalized beyond their times, were nevertheless constantly apprehensive lest they provoke the ill will of gods inconveniently numerous and resentful. Early Christendom raised terrorization to an art; and between astronomical eclipses, the expected termination of the world in the year 1000 A. D., and the undying fire, the imaginative individual had little peace. Death was clothed with terrors unknown to an age producing the philosophy of Metchnikoff, Robert Louis Stevenson, and Walt Whitman. The practical calm of biology has robbed death of much of its terror. Society has more than once had a case of nerves, with the New England sense of exaggerated responsibility achieving no mean distinction in the list.

The practical usefulness of fear is considerable, though the hypertrophied apprehensions and sickening dreads of past ages wrought nothing but havoc. Transferred to situations of actual danger and sublimated from blind panic to rational caution, the fear impulse has constructive possibilities. But it is notorious that uncultivated fear is more likely to attach to inconsequential matters rather than to those of real import. A mouse has still more power to provoke panic than a live wire, and a garter snake than a toy pistol or rusty nails. Germs are not yet feared with a vividness comparable to that experienced in the presence of small creatures of fur and feathers. Civilized man needs to know what not to fear and what to fear. Old wives' tales are in competition with science here. Instinctive fear of the dentist is too strong, while the fear of death should, even in its rationalized and attenuated form, exceed that of going to a hospital.

The teaching of safety first, begun by industrial concerns and extended by instruction in schools, is a deliberate effort to build up useful fear. The wide prevalence of accident situations in modern life amply justifies the emphasis placed upon preventive fear. One does not fear effectually, unless informed. To know what harms and what is innocuous tends to build up appropriate emotions. Vice, seen as a monster, inspires terror. Loathing, fear and horror, which medical and social science are laying the fact foundations for, in dealing with sex diseases, are capable of assuming proportions of great efficiency. Our organization of fears is much askew for maximum social welfare. There are fears that need to be reduced and extirpated and fears that are as yet inadequate for welfare. Christian Science has done well to perceive the need of using the soft pedal on fears of a kind. But there is just as much need of inspiring fear to right ends. Emotional cultivation, the most enigmatical and neglected kind of culture, has no larger problem than to appraise and regulate fears.

Fear of impending social calamity, a fear which may have inspired the virulent attempts to reduce the heretic by torture in the dark ages, may be wholly misguided. The social alarmist imparts a subtle terror that may take the shape of persecution and panicky reversion. There is such a thing as social stampede. The meaningless fright that causes herds of horses and cattle to stampede is paralleled in society. The witchcraft delusion was a human stampede. The sinister unanimity of the stampede and the fear that drives the mob are opposed by better fears—the fear of being unjust, the fear of denying rights guaranteed by law, the fear of harming society by closing avenues of invention and inspiration, the fear of being found in the booby trap.

There are few individuals who do not suffer from too much fear, and there are probably none whose fears are suitably distributed over the field of menace and are neither exaggerated nor inadequate. Possibly fear is largely a transitional phenomenon —an expedient on our way to fuller civilization.

Nature places reproduction squarely upon an instinctive basis. In sex the war between reason and social well-being on the one hand and blind impulse on the other is equaled in violence in no other department of experience. Reason is a later and higher nature, so the conflict is between slight reason and more reason, between blind instinct and instinct touched with reflection.

Instinct would fill the world with populations fighting for food and held down to low levels of squalid conflict. An interplay of increasingly regulated instinctive forces has moved mankind toward the monogamic family and adequate care of the young. With well-organized individuals in well-organized society, initial sex interest is substantially succeeded by rationalized parenthood and altruistic social enterprise. Undeveloped interests, obscene or prurient literature, underpay and poverty, which delay or prevent mating, and lack of vision, unite to arrest the evolution of the higher expressions of sex in society.

The flowering of the parental form of sex instinct

in the pride and care of children signifies much in human evolution. The parental interest has entered upon a career of symbolic creativeness. No former age ever saw such sustained and devoted nurture of the young. Symbolic parenthood is exemplified in the socially creative effort of humanitarians and teachers.

The family is significant in social organization, for its ethics and regimen are types and patterns of the larger institutions and ideals of society. However, there are families and families. There is the monarchical family, found especially in monarchical countries, where the children and mother are subjects. There is the democratic family in which there is the ideal of self-government and joint obligation. Whether the state derives from the family or the family copies the prevailing governmental example may not always be clear; presumably the examples are mutually influential. In the family, however, it is possible to develop the attitudes and practice that lie at the threshold of higher social organization.

The sense of social interdependence and justice originates and finds exercise in the rationalized family. Demarcation of individual will is involved. The franchise, balloting and committee procedure are illustrated, as well as the function of law. The advantages of skill and education, of self-restraint and truth-telling, are impressed upon the mind.

The conception of society as a family and the organization of society on a family basis have characterized all societies. It was thus with the early Hebrews and with the village communities of India. Family psychology supports the Japanese throne. The last Tsar of Russia was the little father of a large number of adult children who got out of hand. Our Red Indian wards have been wont to address the "great father" in Washington. It appears there are fathers and fathers. But at the basis of society is the family; it is the fundamental unit of government and group. Families of the most diverse character have much in common as have governments the most diverse. The more liberal, scientific and specifically democratic the family, the better adapted it is to afford to general society preformed materials for higher civilization. The democratic culture of the family needs but to be generalized to impart its character to all social institutions.

Our inherited tendencies are by no means precisely adapted to the environment of contemporary life; indeed, it is likely that at no time in the past have instincts ever functioned with great nicety and without incidental harm. At any rate, these fundamental tendencies are significant to-day as sources of motive rather than as guides to program. Constant oversight and direction are required to shape the expressions of instinct to constructive and beneficial ends.

XI

THE CREATIVE ASPECT OF PLAY

The present recognition of play in the education of the young and in the activities of adults of all social classes is both in quantity and quality a unique phenomenon. When school systems affecting millions of children base procedure upon the free activity of play, and when millions of adults, representing not only the moneyed class but the industrial worker, adopt play as a part-time employment, there is reason for reflection. We still meet the man who never takes a vacation and the person who has the unquiet servile conscience; but on the whole it can safely be said that modern life takes to play with singular catholicity and a rich material equipment. The play ideal in the school is a frank innovation, and the play of adults is as frankly a departure from the approved conduct of large numbers in times past.

Play, instinctive in man and lower animals, is an impulse from within which finds expression in obviously inherited movements. Thus the kitten chases and pounces upon a spool in a manner that testifies to the mouse-catching activities of untold generations of cats and their untold generations of catlike ancestors. The kitten rehearses family history. But in rehearsing the activity the kitten prepares for the future, for it will catch mice and red squirrels as occasion offers. The animal's play is evidently pleasurable. One can be sure of play by the joy unconfined. The passing of energy along the routes established by old wont is uniquely gratifying.

The human play tendency similarly recapitulates ancestral activities and serves to develop needed skills. The child plays imitatively, yet all his play activities are readily referred to types of ancestral activity. The exact form of instinctive expression is only generally predetermined. Hence the copying of the activities of older children and of the occupations of adults is pronounced.

The reversion to old types of motor activity is attended by deep emotional satisfaction. Play releases funds of emotion whose origin is remote. The use of muscles in racially old ways in the free circumstances of recreation gives vent to the inherited nature of man. Sports and games select and organize ancestral types of activity. The ball game is a substitute for many of the features of primitive combat and chase. The ball is symbolic of the hurled missile or the weapon sent to bring down game. The running and evasions, striking the ball, even the uncouth clamor from the bleachers, make an appeal to the primitive within us. Clan and tribe are symbolized in the opposing teams.

Modern life is built so athwart many of our strongest tendencies that to go back into the past through play is like taking a cool plunge on a hot day. The knotted tensions and restrained powers of the normal inheritance find soothing and delightful relief in the comparatively rude experiences of the bowling alley and the hand ball court. Absence of ultimate design, and relief from serious calculation and sustained thought, are characteristics of play. Point by point play shows contrasts to the vocations men live by. A wide range of unconventional conduct, from sports and games to the bizarre diversions of drunkenness, war, and kleptomania, is referable to tendencies that were present in the lives of our crude ancestors.

While play derives its motives and to a large extent its forms from racial reminiscence, and its gratifications are the old delights of rudimentary society, it is an experience that carries certain possibilities of future usefulness as a social factor. The spirit and attitude of play and the contacts and liberations associated with play have no small promise as affording conditions of social progress.

Play carries with it an extensive culture for the enjoyable use of leisure and thus effects a transfer of attention from production to consumption. It signalizes the passing over of society from the pain and famine basis to that of substance and plenty. Associated with rising wants and standards of happiness, play in adult society serves to stimulate more intelligent and abundant production as a means of realizing cultural needs, which are rarely satisfied without considerable attendant expense. The present industrial period is characterized by spasmodic and throttled factory production, by absurd and wasteful duplication, by disregard for regional economies of production and transportation, and in general by a social anarchy of production, shot through with singularly successful selfish effort to amass wealth. The elephantine confusion of society in regard to achieving a maximum of economic well-being, and the keen directness of the private corporation to obtain corporate enrichment stand in sharp contrast. It is possible that the widely developing play-interest will supply incentive to cause production to enter upon a more coördinated and fruitful career. Of course, as it is to-day, the constant piling up of rather permanent forms of wealth, as in improved lands, bridges, buildings, jewelry, technic and education, makes each succeeding generation richer than the last. Inheritable wealth keeps mounting to higher and higher levels. More people inherit wealth and each on the average inherits more than was formerly possible. Disorganization of money systems may give a temporary appearance of poverty, but the essentials of wealth were never so plentiful before.

Along with increase of material means of satisfying wants, there thus appears a recreational tendency which looks toward a fuller life and ultimately higher culture standards. Thus play, whether in all cases well chosen or not, stands in lieu of a kindergarten for raising the masses to an acceptable plane of consumption. By trial and error, by silly amusement and raucous violence of athletics, the people become accustomed to the problem of living in plenty and feel their way toward the arts and amenities that can appear only in an environment not dominated by gross toil and severe necessities of production. The play instinct, finding expression in whatsoever present forms, is the potential source of fine and finer arts, of the flowering of creative talents.

To the city dweller outdoor recreation is a release from the confinement of employment and the restrictions of an artificial environment; it releases tensions and restores to a normal simplicity. Country life of the unsophisticated type is, however, stimulated and socialized by recreation. In both the case of urban and rural life, play performs the function of supplementing the usual experiences of occupations and results in enlarging the personality—a contribution of great importance. So strong an appeal is made by sports and games that some vigilance is required lest excess of diversion betray both industry and the achievement to which the play experience conduces.

The mental and physical limitations imposed on the individual by most modern employments are suspended in recreation. Herein lies a special value of play. In adult life the play instinct serves peculiarly well, as it does notably in childhood, to give confidence, and release expression for latent powers. The muscle-bound farm boy feels more competent and independent for having learned tennis and dancing. The middle-aged woman who learns to swim or drive a car takes on an access of personality and self-respect. Recreation and avocation have marked power to make people think well of themselves—and when they do that, the outlook for democracy improves. By preserving through play a plasticity like that of infancy, the adult becomes more versatile and efficient in all relations. Youth is a high condition; by play, with its demand for mobility and adaptability, the adult fends off the encroaching death of habit and factitious respectability. Obsessions, dogmatisms, finality and festering memories find difficult footing in minds made inhospitable to their presence through rich experience in the free activities of play. The dwarfing of natures through being shut off in childhood from normal play is well known. The child that has not played lacks in development; not less does the adult suffer who loses the impulses that go with spontaneous and wide-ranging mental and motor activity.

Denied free expression in acceptable forms, in the child and the adult, the play instinct may find invidious outlets. A study of youthful criminal tendencies of a number of reputable citizens, by Professor Swift, brought out the fact that in nearly every case these individuals, including business men, lawyers, teachers and others, showed such tendencies in early life. The offenses reported ranged from setting fire to buildings to stealing fruit from farmers' trees, and from ineffectual attempts to kill other children to heaving stones at widows' houses. Nearly every one will plead guilty to the charge of having done irregular and incipiently criminal acts in childhood and youth. These ill-conceived acts, instinctive all, can be culturally replaced or fanned into criminal career. The whole scheme of civilization is one for the replacement of antisocial, with social, forms of expression, of substituting wholesome conduct for that which is instinctively prompted to evil results. Games, sports and avocations are prophylactic measures of outstanding value. The phenomenal influence of physical diversion and training to rectify conduct in schools and colleges is well understood by administrators of education. Problems of discipline, as they were encountered in days of preachy restraint, have practically disappeared in such institutions—thanks to the substitutional efficacy of athletics and the gymnasium.

The motivation of professions and occupations, whether from slavish compulsion or from sheer delight and interest, is closely related to personal happiness and the future of society. The excellence and quantity of product are affected by the worker's motives, but particularly is his attitude the measure of his fatigue, content or discontent. Lack of suitable motivation, lack of recognition that the state of mind of the worker is a most important fact, not only affects production in quantity but insidiously influences quality and range. With the releasing motives of play operating in the world's work, astounding advances would be made. A person who does not like a job will not give it enough thought and patience to bring out its latent possibilities. Invention and finish spring from spontaneous, playlike, appetitive devotion to one's employment. Brusque indifference to the imponderables gives modern industry and employments a crudely mechanized and art-lacking character. In the psychological conditions of vocations lies the possibility of artlike production and, indeed, the possibility of turning the industries into fine arts. Here and there is a farmer, a stock-raiser, a florist, or a teacher who is motivated for art rather than for job. But such appear to be exceptional. Neither in immediate character of employment—in its associated ideas—nor in features of variation and progression does the vocation ordinarily make one tenth of the appeal made by taking part in dramatics, or playing "first base" on an improvised baseball team. The arts have stood off by themselves as unique adventures in the creative mood. It would be strange if in all the diverse vocations of modern society there were not to be found ample space for analogous creativeness and devotedness. If the usual employee were to declare that he loved his work, his fellows would snort.

We could get along with even less production, if necessary, provided employment were better contrived for motive, though increase of production would doubtless ensue from cultivating the art or play motive. There is no more pregnant enterprise than that of a better motivation of industry. How retarded such enterprise is may be inferred from the amazement of novelty that greeted Carleton Parker's discovery that the complex of restiveness of the I. W. W. of the Oregon lumber camps was causally related to the wifeless state of the members of this organization.

The craving for playful change finds satisfaction in travel and vacations. By entering new environments the individual is subjected to much the same demands for mobility that are afforded by play. The developmental influence of travel—of any radius—for any purpose, affiliates with that of play, in that it entails new adjustments and breaks up conventional attitudes. The harmonizing of the socially diverse is hastened by modern means of travel. There is a close connection between the mating impulse and the interest in travel, as witness the frequency of marriage of persons of different geographical association—intertribal as it were. Fixedness of concept and avoidance of the problem situations from which reason springs are scarcely possible to the person whose horizon is widened by adequate and significant travel. Whatever comes to the world, we may be sure that our time is decisively marked off from preceding centuries by the steel rail and the ubiquitous automobile. There are no historical parallels for a civilization that witnesses the possibility of setting free the individual from the limitation of place and of stimulating through novelty and comparison.

Avenues of social welfare open along the route of more natural and spontaneous motivation in industry and of greater recognition of the interests represented by play. Industry, though highly mechanized, need not inevitably mechanize the worker. The organization of work to present continuing appeal to curiosity and adventure is possible. Recognition of the need of improving motivation in the different employments would go a long way toward inspiring the social invention necessary for bringing about its realization.

The larger use of the great natural playgrounds of the world, freer access to them through adequate and inexpensive transportation facilities, and the liberation of pent-up urban populations to contact with nature are easily possible, lacking only determination to put material assets to social uses. An emboldened spirit of play might prove to be the world's highest wisdom.

Yet there is triumph for play. Mark Twain declared that man's supreme weapon, unused, is laughter. Books have been written on laughter, and the circumstances of this type of expression have been documented to a degree. Laughter belongs only to man; it is aroused only by man or manlike animals or things; it cannot be provoked by inanimate nature; it is an expression of self-superiority in view of the blunders of inferiors; it is symbolic defiance; it originates in happy surprise—as anger comes from unhappy and sudden obstacles; it is like stepping down two steps of stairs instead of the expected single step. Physically, the expression of laughter mimics the glad and mouthful expression of a dog making toward a bone and evincing a state, translatable into the words, "It is good, I will eat it." Such are some of the explanations of laughter.

Laughter witnesses to a sense of suitability and a perception of the incongruous; therefore the mind that laughs must know alternatives. With ideas uncompared no one would laugh. When a man has only one idea, that idea is as serious as can be; when he laughs he is virtually saying that he has had another idea. By laughter one also suggests that others possess themselves of different ideas. Napoleon's soldiers apparently always took the oratory of their hero seriously. Suppose they had snickered. Men have been known to break up meetings by laughing at the wrong place. A supreme weapon of emancipation, a unique defense of defenses, an irresistible force is laughter.

The variations of experience induced and gratified by the play instinct tend to yield the net result of fitting the individual for more happily taking his part in society. Whether play be regarded as an expression of surplus energy, or as a recapitulation of race experience, or as a form of preparation for later activities, it contributes notably to ideal social qualifications.

XII

SOCIAL USES OF MEMORY

The function of memory is to provide the individual with useful images of past experience. Its function in the individual's public mind is to recall former events of significance for social welfare. In common with other memories the citizen has a store of materials relating to history and social developments. What store he possesses depends upon factors of recall. These factors, subject at all times to interest as a superior selective influence, are vividness, primacy, recency, and repetition.

Vividness has reference to the definiteness and depth of original impression. If one has been in a railroad accident, he finds that the circumstances and details are vividly impressed and not to be forgotten. The fright and terror of accident serve to impress images ineffaceably. Great joy or pain stamps impressions permanently upon the nervous system. Pain is to be avoided in the future and joy is to be sought; hence the accommodation of memory. Early settlers in the lower Hudson River valley had the custom of "whipping the boundaries." Land boundaries consisted of natural objects, as a basswood tree, a large rock or a convenient stump. One farm was marked off from another in this manner. It became necessary to remember boundaries. So the boundaries were "whipped in." The children would be given sound whippings at the boundaries; the natural objects thus serving as demarcations and their significance were deeply impressed by the accompanying stimulation. This was vividness. As a compensation for this barbarity, the children, let us believe, never failed to inherit the goodly acres undiminished, though whether, as Freudians might contend, there ever after was a fear of approaching boundaries, remains a question.

First impressions are lasting; primacy of experience gives memory a firm attachment. One remembers well how a person looked when first seen, how a place appeared when first observed. Later images may be blurred, but the original experience remains in clear outline. The clear memories of childhood benefit from the tenacity of the cells of the brain for original and primary impressions.

Experiences of later years have not the same strength of attachment. A prophet is without honor in his own country because his elders cannot forget his boyhood, cannot think of him except as somebody's unprophetlike son. If George Washington, to the schoolboy, had the congenital defect of being unable to summon to his aid the most inheritable of defenses, the schoolboy can scarcely ever afterwards listen to fresh evidence or revise his conviction on Washington's singular disability. Having in mind thus the peculiar effectiveness of first impressions, we should feel less indulgent toward the practice of permitting first impressions to be incorrect.

At the opposite pole from primacy is recency as a law of memory. The most recent impression is also lasting. We remember not only how John looked when we first saw him but also his last appearance before he marched away; last views cling. We are not powerless under the spell of first impressions; the last pretty face, alas, has its spell. There is much in position. Of ten candidates for office we remember the first we heard speak, remember distinctly, and we remember the last also distinctly, for he was the last. The intervening eight, other factors being disregarded in the illustration, are less definitely recalled. A candidate might, however, have a superior claim on memory for having been the beneficiary of some special factor of vividness.

There is an element of instinctive economy in this dominance of first and last impressions. The mind shirks the labor of comparison and equity. It is easier to make up one's mind and let it stay made up on first impressions. By mentally giving the prize to the first speaker the burden of judicious assessment of values is avoided; and, with the last impression, it is the easier way to give the last speaker a preference than mentally stage a parade of all the preceding claimants for honors. The mind seeks the path of least resistance with the placid indolence of a stream of water running down hill. What strategies for getting in the last word—and with what good reason! The vote of prejudice is easier than that of thinking.

Playing across the foregoing factors, like a thread in a fabric, is repetition. Great is the power of the repeated word. Repetition dominates among the factors of recall, for the repeated idea is sure at some time to be first or last or to be timed with moments of vividness and emotion. If a thing is said a hundred times the chances are that at some time it will make a strong appeal; it will find a joint in the armor. After sleeping through a barrel of sermons, the parishioner may wake to hear a direful prediction and straightway beg for mercy. Repetition has an inclusiveness like the charge from a shotgun. Advertising makes use of all factors of memory, but use is especially made of the law of repetition. Even falsehood wins with repetition, for vigilance can be tired out. Deny the repeated statement, flout it, disprove it, yet with its repetition there is beaten up a dust which settles like an opiate over denial. With repetition as a method even dullness becomes leadership. The keen mind may tire of reiterating the same idea, leaving to those who are calloused to repetition the necessary service of saying things over and over for twenty five years, until the majority are caught awake.

Much that is experienced is not retained; a mass of items to which we give little or no attention, or heeding, do not remember. As attention is selective, like a bee visiting only certain flowers, so are the preservations of memory but fragmentary. Governed by interest we give heed mainly to what is significant at the moment; and thus is memory as full of gaps as were our earlier attentions and interests.

But in addition to the selection by interest, we

have in the operations of memory a selective ejection of what at one time was heeded and stored in memory. Disuse and aversion unite to empty the memory of incidents and details. In the main we recall things that are of use and forget the useless. The operation of the mind is not perfect in this regard, but the principle is demonstrable. Forgetting, it must be said, is not quite what it should be. We go madly about because we have forgotten the unforgettable and think of things we should not. The things actually blotted from remembrance are not always what an unbiased jury would recommend, and the things retained are oftentimes of dubious serviceableness.

Selection, retention, and forgetting have special significance in matters of social program. Society is as much a creature of social memory as is the individual responsive to his own remembered experiences and the principles derived therefrom. What is recalled of society, for society, determines in effect what kind of civilization shall ensue. Just as the individual without memories would proceed by instinct mainly and thus differ widely from cultured man, so society divested of history and precedent would approximate primitive barbarism. Present-day society is founded upon the truth and falsehood delivered to us by the fathers, and incremented by socially memorable instances of recent origin. Social memory goes back as far as history and tradition. Well may it be said that we are the true ancients; historically, we have the longest memories.

The nature of the content of social memory is determined by interest, attention, and forgetting, as in the case of the individual memory in matters of individual import. An important rôle is played by those who select for the sociai mind, and who help it to forget. The author and the historian are from this viewpoint social architects, as are likewise the lawyer, clergyman, and teacher.

Individual well-being is closely bound up with selection by memory, depending on what one remembers and what one forgets. The person who remains too conscious of past mistakes and too alive to former animosities and hatreds is limited indeed. It is necessary to forget. "Forget it" is an admonition of considerable wisdom. The mind that constantly reverts, reverts comprehensively, is not the happiest or most promising type. A convenient "forgettery" is as valuable as a good memory. We read of people who live next door to each other for years divided by a spite fence—and we recall the history of Alsace-Lorraine. There is culture that is almost wholly retrospective. One must live out of the past, it is true, but such fullness and tenacity of indiscriminate memory as make the future uninteresting and the present opaque is a downright misfortune.

The rôle played by history is therefore wholesome or the reverse according to the stressing of materials. On the whole it can safely be said that the world suffers from history. No one can be in the city of Boston without feeling that Boston suffers from history; it benefits from history, to be sure, but it also suffers from it. France and Germany suffer from history; they will suffer from it as long as they will not forget and begin again with relieved minds.

In a measure the historical past should be neglected. We treasure the details of evil precedent at our peril. The historical way becomes the easiest way. In time of crisis, the old vicious precedent being at hand, the mind effects a tragic economy of effort by reversion to practice. With less knowledge of how our forefathers behaved, we should ascend to solutions based on reason and foward-looking considerations.

But perhaps it is not the facts of history that are opposed to progress so much as it is the spirit of acceptance and deference. History is not recorded dispassionately; such a thing is impossible. Bancroft wrote history to justify the ways of God to man, and A. M. Simons writes it to demonstrate economic determinism. The earlier school histories of the United States were written to brand the redcoats and to instill gun patriotism. Dr. Beard prepares textbooks that bring to light the achievements of the plow and the dynamo, the microscope and the blowpipe. Carlyle made a god of Napoleon, and H. G. Wells shows him as a contemptible, energetic, but not incomparable devil. The traditional idolizing of Napoleon by the Frenchman could no more exist in the presence of *An Outline of History* than reverence for Cotton Mather can exist in the mind of the reader of the Massachusetts Historical Society's letter written by Mather, hopefully referring to a possible capture of William Penn at sea and his sale as a slave to the West Indies. Propaganda is implicit in the very constitution and temperament of the historian and in the necessity of selection. Find a writer who has no point of view, no sentiments and prejudices, no emotions, no cultural background, no personality and no mouths to feed, and we may then search for the historical volume free from bias.

Historians have dropped the curtain on the horrors of the Inquisition. This precedent may well be followed in other matters. There is always danger lest what is cited for warning shall be perverted to serve for imitation. Modern society may very well have its attention diverted from much in history, and where not oblivious to it, a modern interpretation should be fairly indicated. It is of the greatest promise that fresh organizations of historical materials and compilations of newly unearthed facts are undertaken, and that history is not allowed to rest under interpretations put upon it by writers of former generations. The interpretation is the thing, for it is the emotional influence of the interpretation rather than facts given without inference that determines whether history shall prove a drag or an inspiration.

The dynamic quality of new countries is due to the meeting of difficulties for which precedents do not exist, and to exemption from history. The new country is lacking in monuments, and its place names are not directly associated with historical happenings. Something is lost in richness of associations, but something is gained in sweep and freedom. A picturesque stone railroad station of early date in an eastern city inspired local residents with sentiments of regard. Reading the date, a man from a "new state ejaculated: "Time they had another."

Progress comes with the breaking of old ties, with the shedding of the cast of custom, with escape from the spell of environment which in due time makes black and white rather indistinguishable. The claims of tradition come to outweigh considerations of equity and efficiency; the luxury of habit leads through conservatism to degeneration. Not a little of the world's advance has come from men who were considerably ignorant, not knowing how impossible were the achievements they set out to do and realized. The greatest social lethargy may be found among persons of endowment whose nerve has been refrigerated by the cultures of precedent—etymology, Perry's common law pleading, the novels of Sir Walter Scott, creeds and ancient commentary, and the five-foot shelf. If the ancients were alive again they would come to us in droves to learn wisdom. Marcus Aurelius would properly look upon John Burroughs as a man-child regards his father driving the car.

In recognition of the laws of memory the first learning of history should be impartial as may be and as constructive, first impressions being scrupulously guarded. The world has a chance to begin all over again with the life of every child; and unprofitable attitudes brought down by argumentative history can at least be avoided in the first impressions of childhood. What the English are to-day, and what modern conditions of trade and intercourse are, signify far more to the Irish than the England of Cromwell's time. An auspicious beginning can be made by emphasizing conditions to-day, with liberal recognition of the probability of future change. To plunge the child into ancient and oftentimes malforming culture materials when he is of nascent eagerness of memory is to fix his ideas and form his mind too much in the likeness of his progenitors.

The factor of repetition can be utilized better through lessons embodying socially constructive ideas than through drills that reiterate items of dynastic and presidential chronicle. The character of China was determined by the fact that its youth had long been restricted to the formulae of the Confucian classics. To apply repetition in the interests of progress requires selection of dynamic thought materials.

The force of recency as a factor in the operation of memory—the power of the final admonition and the last word—is recognized in a variety of situations in home and society. But the last word, the most recent utterance, the pursuing, inescapable utterance is from the newspaper. What sort of last word, of ever-recurring last word is this? It would be well if the last word were the best considered, for it is this that often decides policy; well if the social mechanism for repetition were to charge memory again and again with the highest thought and purpose. Our recollection is not too often refreshed with the world's greatest thoughts.

Vividness, as a law of memory, can be extensively utilized for socially constructive effort. The vividness of dramatization has large possibilities of usefulness in social service. Much of the most vividly presented materials to-day have slight social value. On the other hand, much of the news and principle that is socially potent is not found in large type or in the movies. Science, philosophy, literature, social and economic fact, synthetic history, industrial pioneering and dynamic psychology all might largely share in appeal to memory through vividness of expression. Pictures, bold-faced type, and emotional portrayal can be harnessed to social welfare as well as disproportionately employed upon trivial or diverting subjects. A circus means less to a town than does city planning, but one would not infer this from the amount of ink used. The heaviest advertising is by no means that in behalf of civilization by design.

XIII

THE ART OF ACCURACY

Progress is largely determined by the fields of observation entered and by the fidelity of search and exactness of report upon things perceived. Less error arises from faulty functioning of the organs for receiving impressions than from faulty inference and generalization. The belated arrival of impartial and scientific interpretation of phenomena cannot be laid at the door of any deficiency of sense organs, but rather is to be ascribed to obtrusions of preconception and prejudicial theory.

Exact observation is not only the basis of physical science but it is likewise the foundation for social welfare, of which physical science is so large an element. Thoroughgoing, circumspect, and untiring observation over wide fields is an essentially modern practice. Upon its still greater popularization and extension depends future progress. A list of modern sciences is a list of the fields wherein the method of circumspect and unfettered perception has made headway. The pseudo science and misinformation of early times represent taboos on scope of observation or faulty procedure. Welfare is favored especially by carrying over to the social field the ideals of perception that have brought success in the understanding of natural phenomena.

Instead of being easy, veracious observation is the most difficult of feats, and the most unusual; it amounts to genius. To shake off prepossessions, to discount previous impressions, and to look with fresh eyes of truth is a triumph of mental skill. Few achieve it; few try; few have any doubts about the self-acting and wholly satisfactory conduct of perception when left in its natural state. That the intake of impressions is a sluiceway of misunderstanding is inconceivable to those who have given the matter no thought. We see what we wish to see; we glance and then retreat to luxuriate in memories. Believing in premonitions we ignore the hundred exceptions and shout with glee of faith confirmed, when a hit appears to be scored.

No duty is so imperative, for individual or society, as that of stripping the observational process down to working efficiency. We are lost indeed if we fumble in observation. We do not try to see with the ears or smell with the kinesthetic sense; nor should we try to see with eyes blind by suggestion, prejudice, and taboo. The precise and delicate skill required to glean the truth is a culture in itself.

An encouraging wariness, with reference to hasty generalization, is an outstanding fact of the past few years. There is coming in the world a distinct tendency to evade the burden of too great assumption. This trend is observable in political, business and philosophical circles. There is much less cocksureness than prevailed formerly. It is as if the problems of society had become too intricate for hasty judgment and dogmatism. This scientist-like pose is highly auspicious. Learning to say "we do not know" marks an advance. This attitude lends itself to inquiry, and out of teachableness come social advance and prosperity. Men in administrative positions increasingly show this saving grace. High qualifications for office are plentiful culture and information, kindly democracy, a tentative constructive program—and confessed ignorance. No highly desirable candidate knows twenty-four hours in advance how he can vote on all questions.

With conviction regarding possibility of error comes a greater appetite for ascertained data, statistical information of impartial character and the findings of persons better experienced than ourselves. One of the social triumphs of science has been the creation of a demand for information. To a large extent this demand is, popularly, for information upon production. In agriculture and the industries tradition is being supplanted by exact information. Taught to call upon the laboratory or research staff for facts of production that spell success in vocation, the citizen tends to move out of the field of credulity in other matters. He realizes that his political representatives cannot well act without reliable reports. The function of commissions is respected; the survey is taken for granted. We are not likely to overestimate the immensity of social change implicit in the distribution of scientific data among the masses. Rationalizing the familiar employments widens into rationalizing the social process. The time will come when birth control can be discussed.

With the growth of interest in information and inquiry, language tends to be freed of resounding but meaningless phrases, and the spell of words to fail. The word is scrutinized and realism appears in the details of literature; oratory declines. The attaching of meanings to words is attended by greater watchfulness.

Superficial and inexact ascription of meanings

is correlated with hazy perceptions and slouchy method. Numbers of words that have played important rôles in history have been essentially undefined—defined without exact perceptual discrimination. Hence it comes about, that, if one declares his allegiance to words his allegiance in fact may not be questioned. To probe the fitness of words is to detect reality, and this is the peculiar merit of scientific procedure. The cloaking of meanings and production of illusion through verbalism has been one of the besetting sins. The complacent use of partly understood words, while giving contentment of knowledge, is one of the effective forms of ignorance. Acceptance of literary materials in lieu of perception of the verities, which language is supposed to reflect faithfully, gives an aspect of wisdom and learning without their substance. Endless differences appear in the private definitions of words charged with social potentialities. In one person's understanding the word "wealth" may connote the possession of fifteen hundred dollars; in another's a million. To one person old age means to be thirty-five years old; old age to another means eighty. What does honor mean? Honor and dishonor may be found, in individual definition, to apply to the same reality. Agreement on meaning, or, if not this, then declaration of precise connotation of terms lies at the basis of sound popular intelligence. Legislative acts drawn up to contain definitions of special terms used are exemplary in this respect.

The ultimate definition of words is in experience. Meaning is shadowy and unreal except as it is derived from real perception. A dollar earned by the sweat of the brow is a larger coin than one of easy money. Understanding is most complete when there has been actual experience with the realities. No one can use the word "grindstone" with full authenticity without having seen a grindstone, applied the tool, and turned one by hand under pressure. To a person of easy-chair associations a grindstone is an object having dimensions and but little weight or power to tax muscle. Early advocates of trade training for all held, that, by acquainting the upper classes of society with physical toil, the indifference of wealth and leisure to the worker's lot would be diminished. As a basis for social understanding such a program has much to commend it. Social sympathy and the sense of fair play can scarcely develop without a common experience of labor.

An interesting disclosure of the state of mind which is prone to adopt empty forms of words and which prevails in the absence of experience is that of the child who attempts to do things beyond his strength. Every child will propose to do things that he is unable to do. A boy of four has no hesitation in trying to run an automobile. His conceptions of weight and force, of distance and momentum, and of engine power and the resistance of obstacles are so slight that he will attempt to do the work of the skilled driver. Small boys will request permission to use sharp and heavy axes that they can barely lift. Ladders are mounted by five-year-olds in blissful ignorance of the force of gravitation. In hundreds of everyday situations the child, and the inexperienced adult too, for that matter, will reveal an almost grotesque unconsciousness of the qualities of physical objects. The person who has always ridden on rubber tires knows little of what it means to walk twenty miles in a hot sun.

The knowledge possessed by child or adult in the absence of experience is of a weak and watery kind. The limitation of a child's experience appears to be the basis for his willingness to attempt to do the impossible. He has no measure of his own powers, for he knows little of the resistance one meets in trying to do things. The psychology of the inexperienced child was that of Marie Antoinette, who could not understand why the masses starving for bread did not eat cake.

The prospects for the prosperity of truth are compromised because so few of us have any idea of the difficulty of accuracy. Equipped with good intentions we do not realize how naturally fallible are observation and report. Yet accurate observation and statement are extremely necessary for procedure in a hundred different situations where amelioration and justice are at stake. Accurate statement is a fine art. Though we may not at a bound acquire this art, we become at once more desirable citizens by facing the fact that the whole truth is laborious.

The story-telling impulse is strong. There is keener natural desire to be the ballad singer and the great boaster, the applauded wit and potential author of best sellers, than to relate with plodding fidelity. The disposition to turn facts so the silver lining reflects our own glory and distinction is practically irresistible. Moreover, we are not above winning favor, with the powers that be, by editing to placate. The truth—what is the truth? The answer is simple compared to that to the question, the truth—where is it? Who would be so rude as to disagree with others who are convinced, or drop an irritating fact in the midst of peace and unanimity?

Consider the following account from the *Nation*, February 15, 1922:

> Thirty-eight persons positively identified a man in Chicago the other day as an accomplice in a swindle. He was lodged in jail to await trial. There, in the usual course, fingerprints were taken, and were found to vary entirely from those of the real culprit, which fortunately for the prisoner were on file. The man was thereupon taken to court and released, the judge calling the mistake the "most startling proof of human fallibility" he had ever seen. A mistake of that sort may well startle all of us, but it is not as unique as one would like to believe. Lawyers and journalists are alike aware of the uncanny fallibility of eye-witnesses, but juries and the public are still chiefly swayed by this kind of testimony.

In an article, "Certain Defects in American Education," Charles W. Eliot, President Emeritus of Harvard University, recognizes the general tendency to error in statement and report, and suggests educational remedy:

Since the United States went to war with Germany there has been an extraordinary exhibition of the incapacity of the American people as a whole to judge evidence, to determine facts, and even to discriminate between facts and fancies. This incapacity appears in the public press, in the prophecies of prominent administrative officials, both state and national, in the exhortations of the numerous commissions which are undertaking to guide American business and philanthropy, and in the almost universal acceptance by the people at large, day by day, of statements which have no foundation, and of arguments the premises of which are not facts or events, but only hopes and guesses. It is a matter of everyday experience that most Americans cannot observe with accuracy, repeat correctly a conversation, describe accurately what they have themselves seen or heard, or write out on the spot a correct account of a transaction they have just witnessed. These incapacities are exhibited just as much by highly educated Americans as they are by the uneducated, especially if the defects of their education have not been remedied in part by their professional experience. The physician, the surgeon, and the public-health officer often escape these defects, because their whole professional training and experience develop in them keen powers of observation and reasoning, powers which must be generally accurate and trustworthy if professional success has been attained. Some men whose education ceased at fourteen, acquire, through experience in their trade, powers of observation and correct inference which professional men whose education was continued to their twenty-fifth year never acquire. It is the men who have learned, probably out of school, to see and hear correctly and to reason cautiously from facts observed, that carry on the great industries of the country and make possible great transportation systems and international commerce.

Eight years ago Mr. George G. Crocker, a lawyer who had been for several years chairman of the Boston Rapid Transit Commission, and in that capacity had been much interested in lawsuits which grew out of accidents in the tunnels under construction, contrived an instructive experiment on the accuracy of the testimony of bystanders. He invited twenty highly educated gentlemen, all of whom had been successful in their several callings, to witness a brief scene enacted close to them by four actors in about one minute, and to write out immediately, each for himself, a description of what he had seen and heard. Of the twenty witnesses three did not attempt to write out what they had just seen and heard at close quarters. Of the other seventeen no two agreed as to what happened before them, and no one gave a description which was even approximately correct. The group contained one judge, one civil engineer, four business men (active), three business men (retired), and eleven lawyers. Whoever will try a few analogous experiments on groups of his acquaintances will soon learn to distrust all tales which have passed from probably inaccurate mouth to inaccurate ear and on through a series of incompetent transmitters.

The remedies for evils described have already been worked out in a few schools and in the elective courses of some colleges and universities. It remains to apply these remedies universally in all the schools of the United States. These remedies are the substitution of teaching by observation and experiment for much of the book work now almost exclusively relied on; the cutivation in the pupils of activity of body and mind during all school time—an activity which finds delight in the exercise of the senses and of the powers of expression in speech and writing; the insistence on the acquisition of personal skill of some sort; the stimulation in every pupil of interest in his work by making the object of it intelligible to him, whether that object be material or spiritual; the inspiration in every child of tastes and sensibilities which he can use to promote actually his present enjoyment and therefore in all probability his future happiness; and finally the persistent teaching of every pupil how facts are got at in common life, how to make an accurate record of observed facts, and how to draw safe inferences from well-recorded facts. Every boy and girl in school should learn by experience how hard it is to repeat accurately one short sentence just listened to, to describe correctly the colors on a bird, the shape of a leaf, or the design on a nickel. Every child should have had during its school life innumerable lessons in mental truth-seeking and truth-telling. As things now are, comparatively few children have any direct lessons in either process.

Any one who will make the experiment of reading aloud a sentence or paragraph to a group of people and of securing statements as to the content will probably be strongly impressed with lack of accuracy. Normal characteristics of attention and interest as well as untrained powers combine to make report unreliable. Yet the very basis of social well-being is scrupulous accuracy of observation and narration. Much harm is done by unfounded rumors and reports that are not sufficiently attested by evidence. Mob action, unbalanced public opinion, antagonisms, and miscarriages of justice in communities where talk is loose, can be traced ultimately to lack of regard for perceptual truth. As a foundation for social organization the practice of accuracy is second in importance to no other requirement

XIV

THE POWER OF SUGGESTION

To one brought up in cannibal society, with no opposing ideas in circulation, cannibalism would seem just and right. The kind of civilization is determined by the prevailing kinds of ideas. The most abhorrent practices, as for example, the drinking of warm blood from the cut necks of horses strung up by the heels, a Patagonian custom, would look proper to us if this were approved by our elders and we were instructed to this end from infancy. There is little that is inevitable in social evolution; a great deal is due to the ideas that chance to be presented. Man does not inherit any set idea against eating his relatives and neighbors; but a Christian civilization, which is a large body of ideas, forbids. We may not even eat small children, the tidbits of orthodox cannibalism. We may, however, employ them in factories. It is all a matter of ideas. The history of ideas is the history of mankind; modern social conditions are largely a product of suggestion. What ideas rule within the mind, and whether one idea or another pulls the trigger of behavior, is determined very largely by the agencies of suggestion.

Any presentation of ideas to consciousness constitutes suggestion. As conscious or voluntary action is in response to ideas, the determinative influence of suggestion is evident. By control of range and character of ideas presented, virtual control of behavior is ordinarily effected. The control of ideas results in the domination of decisions and actions—as may be readily observed in the conduct of children or in responses of individuals in public meetings. The idea of an act may be regarded as the onset of a force that naturally eventuates in corresponding performance.

The power of suggestion has its root in a tendency of people to economize their efforts and follow the line of least resistance. It is often easier to act than to think; hence an idea that once gains the focus of attention tends to result in corresponding movements and to govern conduct. If a person were restricted to one idea his action could be predicted, for he would have no alternative except to carry out a single thought. Where there is a variety of ideas or suggestions in a given period of time a selection has to be made, as not all can be carried out. The hypnotist controls the behavior of his subject by limiting the latter's field of ideas. Restricted to a single idea, such as that of crowing like a rooster, the subject proceeds to crow; he cannot do otherwise if his mind has only the idea of crowing.

The essential fact to note is that all behavior that is consciously directed is in response to images and ideas. If the idea of murder never entered any person's mind, homicide would cease. If no one thought war, the occupation of the warrior would be gone. The actual selection of ideas determines civilization and governs the individual.

Differences appear in the susceptibility of persons to suggestion, some responding quickly and readily, while others show greater resistance and seem relatively immune. This difference in resistance is correlated with the number and strength of inhibitory ideas, many of which have originated in painful experience. The child is highly suggestible because he has fewer ideas derived from experience to hold against the fresh suggestions. A person whose memory is meager or enfeebled as in sickness is rendered more suggestible, as his remembered stock of opposing ideas is less than normal. But all people no matter how virile and mature are suggestible. One can no more resist the bombardment of suggestions from the press, from history, and from social contact than he can resist the influence of the weather upon his skin. The greatest men of the past have been strangely like the men of their time in most of their ideas and in general outlook; if more advanced in some particulars they have been of the mass in others. The pressure of suggestion is like the pressure of atmosphere, resistless even if not recognized. Li Hung Chang, Chinese viceroy, acclaimed one of the greatest men of his generation, showed in his outlook on life but slight divergence from the prevailing set of ideas of his day and land.

A distinction may be made between positive and negative suggestion. If a person is told not to do a thing, he is given a suggestion of doing it coupled with the suggestion not to do it. In practice the constructive suggestion is better than the negative caution. It is better to say, "Sit up straight," than to say, "Do not sit bent over." The latter form presents the idea of sitting bent over; one has an image of this position, and the negative may not neutralize the improper image. So with the "movie" that shows a burglary of a railroad station, with the burglar ultimately captured and brought to justice; that the burglar is caught may not wholly neutralize the impression left by showing the commission of the crime. Depraved suggestions may be imparted under the guise of moral lessons. Safety lies in the avoidance of the expression of ideas associated with things society does not want done. It is doubtful if preaching against war on the ground of its idiocy and horror would be nearly so effective as saying nothing about war and putting emphasis upon constructive and antithetical measures of civilization.

The early Romans used biography as a source of suggestion. The Roman culture was brought down for centuries by instruction based upon the careers of former statesmen and leaders. Biography is a prolific source of ideals—and its use is capable of forming one generation very much like preceding ones. Literature and history are effective vehicles of suggestion. If literature and history are presented with scientific impartiality and fullness, bad examples as well as the good are brought to attention. Perhaps the scientific historian would oppose obliviscence for masses of historical material, informing, say, regarding the Roman arena, the exposure of infants, and human slavery; but one cannot be enthusiastic over parading suggestions which, carried into action, would plunge us back into barbarism and savagery. At any rate it is a fair inference that there is need of cultivating resistance to suggestion, and, in the case of the young, of noting closely what their reactions actually are to questionable types of culture materials.

It is not possible to know in advance what suggestions will prevail; an example may be imitated or it may provoke defiance. A suggestion that falls in with tendencies is of course much more likely to be acted out than one that goes against desires. In his essay on Liberty, John Stuart Mill maintained that the appearance of drunken men on the streets had a good moral effect as an object lesson for sobriety. There is such a thing as getting wholesome lessons from unworthy examples, but the risk is great. The reaction against the bad example may be violent at first but change later. Given examples of inebriety, the young man might come to regard getting drunk as quite the proper thing, no matter how repulsive the original example appeared. The strange practices of foreign peoples at first strike one as being beyond the possibility of imitation; but no one can be sure that in a given social environment he would not at last quite fully assimilate what at first seemed repulsive and immoral. A man challenged to fight a duel to-day in America would be amused—but not so, in the days of Alexander Hamilton, when the force of this custom and suggestion was so strong that a challenge meant anything except amusement. Up to a little more than a century ago, the suggestion of honor as related to dueling was so pervasively spread through conversation and print that youth grew up locked in a corresponding set of ideas. Then people deprecated dueling and set up a current of suggestion that destroyed the institution.

An example of the effect of suggestion is reported by a man who, as a boy in Iowa, studied one winter an elementary text in American history abounding in military descriptions. Shut in by winter, a number of the boys dramatized military campaigns. One boy would be Grant, another Sherman, another Lee. The excitement of the dramatization was great, and an intense interest in things military sprang from this exercise. The person who reported this childhood experience said that he was inspired with an ambition to become a general and made every effort to prepare for West Point examinations. Several years later he encountered the peace movement associated with the name of Andrew Carnegie and came to have an utterly different attitude toward militarism. Multiply this case by thousands, even millions, and apply the principle to social institutions and practices generally, and one has an explanation for the culture levels of different peoples and periods. The world is what it is to a very large extent on account of basic propaganda and the control of ideas, for ideas determine behavior.

The application of the law of suggestion in health and sickness is noteworthy. One can be made to feel ill by suggestion, and he can be made to feel well by suggestion. It would be attempting too much to expect that suggestion would make a man with a broken leg feel comfortable and whole, but within limits ideas have wonderful power over physical conditions. Patients accustomed to injections of morphine to allay pain are sometimes given without detection a "shot of water" instead. Physicians who have little faith in drugs have found it impossible to practice medicine successfully without some show of medicine bottles, powders, and pills; they lose practice if not sufficiently recognizing the appeal to the imagination of a display of curative agents. Cripples have been known to throw away their crutches under the powerful suggestive influence of sacred shrines and relics. The cheering presence of a well-fed and optimistic physician is often worth more than any medicines he prescribes. But tell a sick person how ill he looks, or advocate the advantages of a sandy soil for burial and the tables are turned.

Of course it will not do to blink facts and deny that evils exist. The emotional response, however, may be directed toward cheerfulness and courage. It is sometimes difficult to decide how far to go in recognizing and denouncing evils, as for example, graft exposures. Take the case of an official who, making purchases for the government, pays a top price for materials and secures an unlawful rebate by dealing with a certain company. Does the description of such a practice tend to honesty or dishonesty? In dealing with matters of this type care needs to be given to the emotional response. The offense would need to be dissected and its bearings shown. The idea that dishonesty is smart would need to be checked by fuller considerations. It is a matter of practical judgment as to how far to go in publicity in dealing with matters of this sort.

A good deal of the discretion required for getting along in society without undue friction consists of a practical recognition of suggestion, lest a casual comment arouse undesired associations. Some imagination is required to say the thing that does not give, even indirectly, an undesired suggestion.

Attitude, dress and manner give suggestions. A cringing attitude invites censure; a confident manner carries with it the idea of success and efficiency. It is often difficult to know when to apologize and how much to apologize. Abject apology may suggest to the injured party that his injury was greater than it was. More than one person has got himself into a tangle by attempting explanations of small matters that might better have been disregarded. The advantage of saying nothing, when that is the best thing to do, appeals to one whenever he notes an example of an unexpectedly perverse association of ideas.

The individual is one person when alone and another when in the presence of others. Let any one turn his mind inward upon itself, and he will discover how changed he becomes by joining with others. Here is a man who in solitude reaches certain conclusions which he confidently expects to urge at a public meeting. He strides zealously to the forum with his convictions bristling. The murmur of the crowd reaches his ear, whereupon he hastily reviews his program of utterance and smooths out a few wrinkles. He joins his fellows and experiences a psychological influence from the antagonistic unanimity of the crowd. His individuality of conviction suffers a strange and sudden shrinkage in the face of massed difference. His ideas, which stood distinct, authentic, and reputable, in solitude, now encounter all the countervailing ideas that an assembly may represent. The invader may now hold to his convictions and declare his faith in the single tax, but he is under strain. His feelings are not what what they were in his study, and his utterance will show dips and evasions and placating phrase. The influence of the many is to strip the individual of individuality and assimilate him into the group. The spell of the crowd may be resisted, but there is no man living who does not become a different person in quality of consciousness when in a group.

There is the compulsion to win the favor of the group. Deep in instinctive inheritance is the need to stand in favor with one's fellows, lest they turn and rend. Man is gregarious and always has been one of the herd—he dreads to be horned out of it and left to batten on the moor. True, he may flout one group, having his eye on some other group for its approval. But every man is playing to a gallery and cannot live without applause.

Spurred by group admiration, the individual will dare what would terrify him when alone. Men in crowds will face dangers and undergo discomforts that as individuals they would flee. Under the stimulus of others' eyes men choose physical hazard as the lesser of two evils, for most men would prefer to risk being killed than to live under scorn. Bathers who would not dream of going into cold water unsupported by mob psychology will affect a fine abandon when of a party of campers. The crowd acts as an anesthetic. The highest type of courage is that of flouting crowd force and opinion. So-called physical courage is as nothing compared with the courage of holding to individual conviction and conduct, with the crowd antagonistic. The crowd is the coward's refuge; the man who is brave only with the pack is the fundamental coward.

Representing a relatively primitive level of mentality and emotion, the crowd supplies ideal conditions for conflagrations of suggestion. Ideas run through compact groups with facility. Such quickness of response and unity of reaction were no doubt conditions for survival in prehistoric ages. A strangely instantaneous unity of movement may be witnessed in the flight of flocks of birds, a flock turning, rising and alighting as if the different members were held together by invisible wires. Something like this instinctive harmony and dominating oneness attaches to man in the mass, with slaughtering effect upon individuality.

Add to the primitive abasement of mob psychology the possible accompaniments of bad air, physical contact, inclosure, fatigue, hunger, and hypnotizing oneness of stimulus, as the silver-tongued, the band, the spectacle—and it becomes a miracle that the tribe has been saved from itself. Happily radio promises to make the building of large auditoriums less likely, and the extension of the ballot to nominations should reduce the number of occasions for crowd orgy in political assemblages.

Something approaching conditions of crowd psychology is implied in the extension of modern means of communicating ideas; but there is the saving factor of interval. Nothing abates crowd psychology so much as a day for deliberation. With time the bowed branches and withered leaves of personal intelligence revive. Anything that makes for delay between suggestion and reaction is therefore a means of grace; time means time to think. Inhibitory ideas come with the dawn; herrings swim across the waters in the meantime. We can be civilized by acting from suggestion, but only from such as the best intelligence certifies.

Conditions that discourage the unanimity of mob mind are auspicious; the opposition of leaders and a diversity of group ideals contribute to the ultimate welfare through affording range for variations of opinion. Free thought came into the world in the gap between the two great branches of the church, a gap which widened into scientific development. Opportunity for social development appears in conflicts of prestige and denials of jurisdiction. It is a happy augury when complaints are heard touching the uncertainties of fashion. That one city rivals another in ultimate authority over what is correct to wear is an advantage. Happy day, when standards are "up in the air"—when no one knows what real poetry is, nor any one knows the ultimate ideals in education, or the true position of women. Inability to know one's place is not without a certain kind of promise; it has the merit at least of preserving us from blasting finality. When there is no one to tell us exactly what to think, we are perforce compelled to think for ourselves.

Convinced of the electrical equality of suggestion, its potency to make behavior and to form institutions, one is impelled toward censorship. But no censorship can prevent partial disclosure, and the surreptitious has strange power to charm. Not in censorship by legal methods can suggestion best be governed for social welfare. The free sifting of ideas, free speech and yet more freedom of speech, free discussion and yet more—these are the means of social safety, just as freedom without stint or limit has been the indispensable condition for the development of science. The scientist is only too ready to disavow a false hypothesis. Yet in the search for economic and social knowledge there is less confidence that the stream will run clear. An error in social theory is as sure of detection and disavowal as a scientific error. The major technic of science can wisely be imitated for social progress. Society can profitably use a larger supply of constructive and rational suggestions and socially salutary ideas. The best way to dispose of a perverse suggestion is to oppose to it a better one, and keep up the process until the people are competent judges of ideas.

XV.

ATTITUDE TOWARD THE SOCIAL ORDER

In theory government is derived from the people, and, in theory, is thus quite secondary to the powers from which it is derived. But there is a tendency for government to harden into a rigid institution and to aspire to social primacy. The continuity and strength of judicial precedent and legislative practice have the effect of making government an ultimate fact rather than a passing phase of social mind.

Established government tends to become too well established, too firmly intrenched through occupation of strategic position. There is rarely in governmental circles as full and free play of ideas as obtains in the more mobile world of general society. Instead of performing the function of agency, government is liable to claim logical priority. True, the right of revolution has been declared, indeed, was declared by Abraham Lincoln; and such assertion shouts the principle of subordination of government to people. But a cross section of government at any time would show that the governing mind is but imperfectly representative of the full social mind, and that often it is not in proper mood to reflect such mind. To achieve a theory and practice of government which will sensitively reflect social development, which will go as fast as the people go, and which will not become in some measure an agency of counter-civilization, is a serious problem. The best ideas, ideas that meet with approval and finally do become part of government, may batter the doors of legislative resistance for years before finding admittance. Woman suffrage, in various countries, the pure food and drugs act, and the income tax law, in the United States, may be cited as examples of the tardiness of legislative compliance.

Society's alter ego, government, may even attempt to snatch the function of forming the popular mind, thus becoming by inversion a commanding rather than a responsive instrumentality. Designing groups may penetrate into government and speak with its great authority to ends that are at odds with the general welfare. Whereas the government should have no mind but the people's mind, there is a tendency for government to declare its mind with intent that the people think the same way. "Eternal vigilance is the price of liberty," spoke the fathers from experience.

The path to welfare lies not through government as a primary agency of social control. Back of government and forms of law are the formulation of opinion and the cultivation of sentiment, of which laws are an expression. Education is a point of origin to law and government; consequently the super-governmental mission of universities and colleges, of thinkers and nonofficial philosophers, may be conceded. It is an ominous condition when it can be asserted that government, in its transient and official character, or any quasi governmental unity, as a powerful financial interest, dominates the means of social enlightenment—that the university, the press, and the pulpit are controlled. If these agencies are not nobly free, they become mere auxiliaries of government rather than contributors to the whole social mind that would employ government as a convenience. A contrast can be asserted between the whole state and the official state, the social state and the mechanized state. It is in the interests of the whole state, the common weal, that agencies of enlightenment be free to exercise the prior rights of investigation and discussion. The distinction between the people and government which was made in the case of Germany some years ago in war time, can be said to exist to some degree in any case. Institutions of learning belong peculairly to the unofficial state and the whole people, and should be unaffected by official mood and unstirred by the comparatively ephemeral governmental organization. The educational function should be separated in control as far as may be from the vicissitudes of opportunist legislation and the fortunes of candidates for public office. It would be well indeed if the whole state, the totality of citizenship, should assimilate the spirit of a self-denying ordinance by noninterference with the processes by which truth is ascertained. There could be no more thrilling experiment than freedom of thought. Education is the most fundamental government.

If there is anything that the busy business man and the laborious laborer needs to know it is how matters stand to-day in the intellectual and scientific world. Even people of some leisure find it difficult to keep abreast of thought developments. Just to know something definite of the data and purposes of organized labor in this and other countries would require considerable effort; and there are men even in public office who do not find time to inform themselves. Nothing short of a straight drive for truth in modern terms will suffice. Similarly with cosmogony and biology. The nonscientific character of much present-day consciousness in these fields is too patent to require argument for more enlightenment. In default of fair-minded introduction to the modern cultures, the pseudo-scientific book and the patent medicine encomium have unwarrantable vogue. Physicians throw up their hands in despair over the ignorance upon vital matters shown by patients. Only the caution of commerce keeps the salesman from fatal amusement over the ignorance of customers with regard to the sources, manufacture, qualities and intrinsic values of goods. Professional men retire to guffaw in concert over revelations of naïve ignorance. The minds of most of us might be better furnished.

There is need of ethical culture fairly based on modern realities; for our emotions of moral approval and disapproval are so little set to the realities of modern offenses of omission and commission, that we are like one who should habitually laugh at the wrong place and shed tears at the authentic joke. "Thou shalt not steal—small sums," says some one. Our consciences antedate big business and modern incitements. The newspapers report severe sentences to prison imposed on young men who steal used cars or forge checks for small amounts. Price jugglings on a national scale, infinitely more harm-producing, easily evade the sentinels of conscience equipped with rusty flintlocks and guttering, tallow-candle lanterns. Forgery has an ominous, common-law sound. Signing certificates of watered stock has no such horrific suggestion. We lack in modern equipment of conscience. When the full circumstances and results of conduct are brought out, when actions are interrupted in the light of all the evidence, there is little likelihood that appropriate social attitudes and revised conscience will not make their appearance.

A few decades ago British workingmen in large numbers followed the scientific instruction in popular form presented by Thomas H. Huxley, Edward Carpenter, and other able leaders. Huxley's lecture on a piece of chalk was a model of exposition on a subject of fundamental scientific import. While the need of exposition in similar fields is still urgent, the greater interest to-day would lie with discussion of social and economic problems. Digestible lessons covering a wide range of unit topics, might prove singularly acceptable to-day, if presented under much the same conceptions as governed the popularization of physical science a generation ago. A wider instructional use is possible of the voluntary or involuntary leisure, always available among millions of adults and young citizens.

Change of popular attitude toward war is among the possibilities. War is waste—waste of wealth and lives. But especially does militarism devastate in the field of mental values; it is a confession of lack of vision and has never attracted men of philosophy and liberal tendencies. Militarism is sterile. The atavism of war brings into prominence and insidiously revives states of consciousness out of harmony with the higher forms of intelligence. Religious and ethical concepts go by the board in war time, and principles of conduct laboriously established among men in private dealings are discarded with the abandon of a Reservation-School Indian returned to the tepee. Theft, lying, homicide, revenge, license, violence—which in peace are outlawed—reappear in the weird relaxation of war. War is a solemn spree imperfectly hallowed by holy names and putative virtues.

It is difficult to express adequately the completeness of antithesis between orthodox militarism, as, say, developed in the Prussian war group, and social program as conceived in the nonmilitaristic mind. A history of the intellectual development of mankind could show no greater contrast than that between the military conception of values and the conceptions identified with education and social science.

Nothing is less implicit in militarism than the democratic ideal. Indeed militarism embalms and hands down as tradition the domination and servility that have characterized caste societies. Feudalism, autocracy, slavery, and the one-man show are implications. The necessity in war for the submergence of personality on the part of the soldier, for his automatization, is at loggerheads with educational theory since Pestalozzi and inverts the emphasis of individual worth asserted by Christianity and given impressive utterance in periods when human rights have been democratically defined. Whereas the aim of modern culture is to bring out personality, military practice represses and standardizes. Ties, associations, ideals, habits, interests tend to be severely erased. It was the purpose of Prussian militarism to reduce the common soldier to an automaton. Success in war would be a high price to pay for the imposition of automatized responses upon society as a whole.

In the light of social evolution the obtrusion of militarism, even when associated with unavoidable necessity on the part of defendant parties, is a deplorable interruption of progress, of the temper out of which progress springs. Any laudable program of social integration or socialization must ever present the strongest possible contrast to militarism, in point of recognition of individual worth and self-direction. It is a debasing experience for society to take on, voluntarily or perforce, temporarily or enduringly, the military mind. The dominance of military groups in society is comparable in principle to supplanting a city commission by its police force.

The fact that wide differences in native capacity exist is a stumbling block to democracy. But ultimate differences are largely due to nurture and education. The inevitable differences in individual ability are probably neither large enough nor distributed in such manner as to conflict with ideals of democracy. The potential intelligence of backward groups and peoples doubtless warrants full confidence in the theory of popular government. Large improvement comes to any mind when it is supplied with ample and suitable thought materials and stimulating opportunity. Through the general diffusion of the best knowledge, and the service of leaders obligated to satisfy a public increasingly rendered critical by education, an approximation to a classless society appears possible.

Whether rational mind shall be limited to class or developed throughout all society is a question that carries with it the issue of caste and slavery. The idea of a return to slavery of the American negro is not extinct, and attempts to destroy organization among the working class would, if successful, amount to nothing less than a step toward the vassalage and serfdom of former times.

The difficulty of abasing to slavery any considerable population would now be great indeed. The possibilities of sabotage are enormous under the conditions of modern labor. At a thousand different points industry is vulnerable to attack. Popular education can hardly be denied, though by an early imposition of narrow vocational training and neglect of quality in elementary schools, as in such rural schools as do not teach reading effectually, the status of a great number could be injuriously affected.

No society is safe that has ignorance and helplessness at its base. Rome might not have fallen had it not been for laws and strategy that undermined the welfare and checked the development of the common people. Democracy and social justice are desirable from every point of view. No social class has any assurance of continued well-being in the absence of welfare in other groups. Universal elevation of standards of living, of enlightenment, of education, and of material prosperity are much the concern of the favored minority. The employer who would break unions would harm society. The individual, unorganized, is unable to hold his own against organization. The competition of group with group is a phase of social evolution higher and more promising than that of individual with group: accordingly the attempt to disrupt and discourage organization among certain classes in society is opposed to ultimate general welfare.

Rational and less rational mind are set against each other at many points. Just as the individual is torn between impulse and reason, so is society thrust one way by reasoned conviction and evidence and turned another by instinct, unreviewed tradition, and force of custom. The welfare of society is bound up with the ascendancy of rational mind.

Every age is an age of reason, but in varying proportions and duration. The dominance of rational intelligence in material progress is an outstanding fact. Rational methods applied to manufacturing, transportation, bridge building, mining, and in all the fields in which modern materialism has made its advance, have been the formula of progress. Scientific and materialistic advance have come in the absence of repressive measures. While the early chemist was regarded with suspicion and the anatomist with horror, for a long time the scientific man has had increasing freedom from interruption by the ignorant and superstitious. Physics, astronomy, chemistry, engineering, and within limits, biology, have been allowed freedom of thought; hence the progress in corresponding fields of material civilization.

But in political, ethical, religious and economic fields, like freedom to grow has not been vouchsafed. It has not been good form to correct inadequate beliefs in these matters with the unsparing criticism that has served to advance science. Higher criticism has been the exception rather than the rule in the social consciousness. Politics and religion have been touchy subjects on which men have shown a temper that would be strangely out of place in chemical research. Experimentation and hypothesis have speeded scientific discovery, while in ethical and economic matters and in law, rational method and criticism have been less employed.

As a result we are adults in scientific knowledge and children in economic and ethical knowledge. We are adults in knowledge of skyscraper architecture, germs, internal combustion engines, thermo-dynamics, histology, long-range guns, submarines, soil physics, and plant pathology. But we are children when it comes to taxation, international concord, public utilities, poverty, unemployment, court procedure, justice and profiteering. The mind has gone ahead where few barriers have been encountered; but in other fields we are still in peevish and childish confusion. We have put away childish things in scientific agriculture and surgery, but we cling to them in relations of politics and economics. Thought is timid and restrained in the laboratory of society, though free and forging ahead in mechanical and scientific fields.

Rational intelligence must extend freely to social problems if it is to equal here its success in the material achievements of our boasted but uncertain civilization. But of even more significance than absolute gains in knowledge is the social attitude. Viewpoint regarding fundamental matters, as war, industry, races, type of government, position of women, and the function of free intelligence, is of critical importance. Again and again must society turn to the clarification and restatement of fundamental principles. In the case of individual career, outlook and trend of thought have controlling influence; so, social attitude and assumption have ultimate importance, for these largely determine the direction of social change.

XVI

AVAILABLE CIVIC ENERGY

The early years of life are of little dynamic value for social organization. The child has neither the interests nor knowledge qualifying him for substantial contribution. His life is largely spent in a series of changes roughly corresponding to the early evolution of man. The lower ranges of human experience engage his activities. He is individualistic, possessing neither the motivation for social organization nor the experience on which social intelligence and vision are based. The immaturity of his faculties is a definitive barrier to contribution to social organization. Vast potentialities lie in the nurture and admonition of youth, in the formation of social mind through specific instruction, family training and the coöperative experience of school and playground and of juvenile organizations. But effective social activity is of course not for the first, fourth or fifth of the span of human life.

On the side of infancy it may be said, however,

that the very ingenuousness of the child reveals clues of no small value for mature society. The happy freedom of this period knows little of class and caste distinctions. The child is the original democrat. His world is one of singularly clear values, freed from tradition and adventitious considerations. Food, relatives, actual conduct, and how things really look, are peculiarly within the child's range of veracity. The careers of St. Francis Assisi, Mark Twain, Jean Jacques Rosseau, Henry D. Thoreau and John Brown, childlike all, suggest alluring "slants" on life derived from infantile characteristics carried over to adult society.

For influence upon language the life of the child affords treasure. If the child's lead were followed, many of the irregularities and monstrosities of book-controlled English would disappear, such as the irregular verb. The child says go, goed; not go, went. He says take and taked: not take and took. His penchant for smoothing away the illogical shibboleths of good grammar is unconventional. Likewise with his unfettered phrasings and impromptu vocabulary. He calls a spade a spade or anything else that it seems to resemble—no small service to language. It has been brilliantly contended by John Erskine that the greatness of Shakespeare as a user of words was from the fact that he spoke with the freedom of the child—thought took shape in words with rare disregard for the dictionary, which, thus fortunately, did not exist in his day. With the coming of the authoritative "unabridged," modern writers are all the time thinking of how they look from behind. Thanks be to Hendrick Van Loon for a whiff of freedom of vocabulary in his *Story of Mankind.* Havelock Ellis, in his *Appreciations,* attributes virtue to Zola for enlarging literary vocabulary by use of terms of the people. Awed by the "unabridged," we fail to assess at their true value the naïve improvisions of the speech of childhood.

There is revisional power, too, in the child's reactions to adults. Many a parent has perforce seen himself in a new light through the reactions and comments of his child. The child unwittingly acts in ways to simulate the effects of the frontier on American mind, producing inventiveness and versatility on the part of parents and adults in the neighborhood.

At the other extreme of life stands the inertia of age—its lessened motivation and completed adjustments. In old age life loses its dynamic attributes. Interest in change and social adventure is diminished. The big, buoyant illusions of early manhood lose their sustaining power. The circle of vision tends to become limited to the routine of familiar business and a safe place for slippers. What matters social reform when, at best, the fruits cannot be enjoyed by the laborer, when, unlike youth, with its assumption of an earthly near-eternity, age knows for a certainty the remorseless haste of the sands of the hourglass?

It is not even a certainty that old age is peculiarly fitted for counsel, if reference be had to the newer problems. For counsel touching matters of long experience old age is especially fitted, though there is the danger of misplaced precedent. The adage, "Old men for counsel, young men for war," implies no improvement on former methods of settling differences. For arbitration and international relations, the counsel of the elder statesmen is not the happiest. There is a tendency on the part of age to put new wine into old bottles, even to deny that the wine is of recent fermentation.

But a cultural extension of dynamic interests and information until very late in life is happily illustrated in the case of many individuals who have tapped the spiritual fountains of youth. The flexibility of a used and frank mind is remarkable in age, while, on the other hand, there are persons of twenty who show the fixation of habit and viewpoint commonly attributed only to advanced years.

The highest point of individual development, viewed socially, is the age, when, with maturity of powers, there is imaginative daring, scepticism of tradition, and ambition coupled with experience that makes aware of the complexity of social relationships and of the difficulty of producing lasting change by violence and revolution.

This intermediate age, in the case of women, is now made especially significant by the franchise. Their civic potentialities are the greater for their relative inexperience and therefore notably receptive attitude and undulled expectations. Their tendency to test institutions and measures by personal effects is of the utmost value to society, for the world has too long been under the spell of institutional formality and solemnity that have diverted attention from painful facts of living conditions. The civic youngness of women provides a factor of spontaneity and significant ingenuousness. The social structure of the future will differ from any before known or possible otherwise than through the presence of the feminine factor in politics.

Not only in civic childlikeness but also in a centering of interest upon child welfare does the woman citizen promise to be a powerful factor in the coming state. The question has historically never been asked in politics, What effect will this measure or that policy have upon the welfare of the child? Non-use of this touchstone has left legislation in the control of one-sided forces. To apply the principle of child welfare means nothing short of a radical reorganization of viewpoint with ultimate revolution of policies. Any public issue, from tariff to good roads, from food laws to prohibition, is viewable in the light of possible effects upon childhood. The woman legislator and the woman voter will be sure to raise the new question. It will be hard to convince mothers, for example, of the necessity of war under any circumstances. Having in mind their hazards of childbirth and their long and arduous experience in securing the physical survival and well-being of their children, they will be likely to agree with General Grant in declaring that there never was a war that could not have been avoided. The enfranchisement of women is likely to prove the turning point between the older state and a revised civilization.

Intelligence in man and woman is a resource which has its limitations as truly as there are limitations of natural resources consisting of coal, oil, or forests. The conservation of intelligence is of the utmost importance. Mind may be undeveloped, misdirected, wasted—futilely employed. The art of civilization involves to a greater degree than heretofore the conservation of mental energy. As the space surrounding a target is larger than the bull's-eye and the chances of missing are vastly more numerous than of making a hit, so the possibilities of error outnumber those of success in the attainment of social ideals. The skillful utilization of limited mental resources therefore is a challenge supreme.

The civic interest is in competition with other interests, and shares, rather than monopolizes, the mental resources of the individual. Indeed it is not of rare occurrence that the civic interest is quite overshadowed. When not overtopped by other interests it is nevertheless limited by conditions of fatigue. The amount of time and energy that the average citizen has left over from private business for the affairs of his city or the business of a board of education, to say nothing of state and federal governments, is oftentimes slight indeed; it is only a feeble fringe. Preoccupation and fatigue are allied for the neglect of civic duty. Especially is it true of factory and mine employees and manual workers in homes and on farms, that there is little energy available for public affairs.

Physical fatigue is directly opposed to interest in the commonwealth, for such fatigue is opposed to the gathering of the knowledge out of which intelligent interest grows. There is a vast amount of actual physical disqualification for intelligent citizenship. The leisured class has usually monopolized politics and managed government largely because of leisure. The makings of civic and political wisdom are not represented by farmers and mechanics who meet late in the evening after the day's work. The singular lucidity of the Athenian Greek's mind and the rare civic perfection of early Athens were not unrelated to the fact that the Athenian citizen was a man who did not know what a day's work was. Democracy will have to find time in the day's program for civic activity. It will not thrive on fragments of time purloined from sleep. In the church of democracy it will not do to have the pewholders snoring beneath the pulpit.

Like fatigue, in representing a factor of civic deprivation, is the modern tendency to give heed only to certain types of experience and information. We have come far since the pansophists of four centuries ago. Francis Bacon took all knowledge to be his province. Men of learning used to blush when forced to admit there was anything they did not know. The attempt was literally to know it all. Milton nearly accomplished the feat. We have decided that it is necessary to know it all simply in one line. The specialist is quite sensitive about revealing any ignorance in his own field, but it seems to detract from the fullness of specialization to be caught with information outside of it. Far from blushing for ignorance of general information the specialist owns up to it or even parades it.

Such contented ignorance might be simply refreshing did it not go so far as to include social science and public questions. But these are included too often; and issues which the citizen is, in democratic theory, charged with finding solutions for in his own thoughts, are lumped together for neglect with knowledge of the other man's specialty. Hence the physician may complacently disavow any interest in or knowledge of public business, and the architect look pained upon being presumed to be interested in a railroad strike except as it means an unwelcome interruption of business.

Such facts and ideals of specialization strike at the very heart of democratic organization. Every citizen should have besides his occupational specialization a civic specialization. Capable or brilliant minds should not be lost to the commonwealth through being penned up exclusively in a profession. Every professional school might properly require a knowledge of economic and social science, of world history and trends of government. The new ignorance should have no standing in modern society. No electrical engineer, dentist, accountant, trained nurse, pharmacist, should be licensed without showing the possession of the essentials of a specialization for efficiency in citizenship under present-day conditions. The candidate who disclosed a dangerous indifference could be advised to emigrate to any country still having a monarchical form of government.

The aversion to becoming an actor in civic business is partly due to the slowness of parliamentary procedure and the laboriousness of the committee. Brisk business men are tortured by the verbose indirection of the city commission or the state legislature. One enters committee meetings with feelings not wholly different from those ascribed by Dante to victims entering the nether region. It is so easy, comparatively, to get things done for oneself by oneself and so devious and irritating to do business with debating clubs. The relative futility of councils and committees is a matter of jest. Congressional method is slow and inefficient. The committee on public business reminds one of the so-called measuring worm that, with its rear body attached to a surface, arches its back and with its claw-equipped front body reaches and feels and tries in all directions for a safe contact, and perhaps makes an end by refraining from forward movement.

Yet laborious and time-consuming parliamentarianism is the only way apparently for liquidating the problems of the myriad-headed public. In private business, outside of corporations, the individual has only one will to express. In public business unreconciled groups and individuals, the community body of the state, press for consideration their conflicting interests; this gives pause. One type of mental product from deliberative assemblies is well represented in pre-election speeches of candidates, which minimize hostilities by presenting platitudes and declaring for propositions that have become extinct through unanimous consent.

The character of legislative procedure is largely due to the guessing of the minds of constituents represented by members. Given a clearer mandate from constituents congresses would fumble less.

Apart from the necessary circumspection of dealing with many-sided issues, the dilatory and lethargic character of collective procedure rests on the curable defect of lack of mechanism for ascertaining majority opinion. Collective deliberation is clouded, too, it must be said, by the psychology of vanity and display. The talkative member is not infrequently more concerned with rhetorical display than with the truth of intercourse and the prosperity of projects.

The work done in parliamentary bodies in the form of analysis through discussion is work that must be done somewhere. The bringing of minds into effective agreement is of fundamental value. The process of making up one's own mind is often slow enough; then how much more deliberate must be the process of forming policy collectively? The making up of individual mind, moreover, is not only slow, but the conclusions which one reaches independently are almost certain to be found faulty in some particulars. One rarely thinks a thing out so fully that he is not compelled to modify his thought when it is subjected to criticism.

The burden which democracy throws upon its deliberative bodies might be lessened by preparatory study and discussion on the part of citizens organized in small groups. A network of clubs for civic study would lay a foundation for a more expeditious disposal of public issues through legislation. Such study of social principles would clear away much of the difficulty that now faces the legislator. In democracy citizenship is a career rather than merely a voting privilege.

A phase of effective citizenship has to do with the conservation of mental resources. Social welfare demands that the individual apportion his energy between personal and community functions. It follows that whatever economies can be effected in vital forces may contribute to socially creative energy. Avoidance of energy-wasting situations is enjoined for personal well-being and for meeting the requirements of a civilization ever becoming more complex.

Energy is conserved by reposeful attitude and the cultivation of relaxation. One occasionally sees a person who nervously rides in an automobile without touching the upholstery at the back, and others who while riding in trains support bundles and packages that could be placed on a mechanical rest without adding to the load of the locomotive. The flexing of muscles and holding them in cramped positions tire. With the arm relaxed the weight is from the shoulder; but with unnecessary rigidity of muscles or with faulty bodily positions the nervous system assumes an abnormal burden with reference to gravitation.

An application of scientific management in the use of one's endowment of energy might make a large contribution to social as well as personal welfare. A multitude of items will occur to one. Excessive talking, the energetic expression of ideas that go by implication, the head-on collisions of disorderly conduct in conversation, might be mentioned. The fatiguing character of worry and fear is everywhere recognized. Not only is fear exhaustive of energy but in many cases serves no purpose, as imagined crises often fail to make their appearance, and the final problem is not one that was anticipated.

Social contacts are of themselves fatiguing, for they are stimulating. Alert attention is provoked by the many new situations that develop when two or more are together. When one is under observation he undergoes more of a nerve strain than when off by himself. To sit or stand in a conspicuous position, to be where others can watch every move, is an exacting experience. Persons who work in offices in full view of passers-by are subjected to a certain strain from this cause. There is little relaxation with full publicity. Hence the value of partitions, screens, ground-glass panes, awnings—anything that will soften the gaze of the observer and afford a suggestion of the privacy of the caveman's cave, the cottage, and the castle.

Predominant employment of the finer muscle represents a special tax upon energy. It is less fatiguing to use the larger muscles of the body and limbs than to do things requiring nice adjustment of the smaller muscles. It is far easier to work in the garden than to write with a pen. Indeed people find their spirits restored by turning from the minute movements of eye and finger to the large movements of play and ordinary physical labor. One of the errors formerly common in dealing with the child and youth was to require an undue amount of work involving close muscular coördination. An example of this is given in *Village Life in America,* by Caroline Cowles Richards. At the age of fourteen, in 1856, she wrote thus in her diary:

Grandmother has offered me one dollar if I will stitch a linen shirt bosom and wrist bands for Grandfather and make the sleeves. I have commenced, but, oh, my! it is an undertaking. I have to pull the threads out and then take up two threads and leave three. It is very particular work and Anna says the stitches must not be visible to the naked eye. I have to fell the sleeves with the tiniest seams and stroke all the gathers and put a stitch on each gather. Minnie Bellows is the best one in school with her needle and is a dabster at patching. She cut a piece right out of her new calico dress and matched a new piece in it and none of us could tell where it was. I am sure it would not be safe for me to try that.

Modern employments abound in kinds of labor involving finer muscular movements. Compare the occupation of the proofreader with that of the primitive hunter or shepherd. The printer's and the tailor's trades outrage a good many of the natural tendencies of man in their restraints upon free and large movements. The accountant whose work is to set down figures and make computations is singularly restricted in his mental activities and no less so in the physical activities associated with pencils, pens, and rulers. A great deal of scientific work, carried on with microscope and laboratory instruments, represents experience quite abnormal when judged from the viewpoint of man's early free state and the vast leisure of pre-civilization.

It becomes correspondingly important to mitigate the severities and nervous strains of modern employments. Change of work, the avoidance of monotony, shift of physical position and limitation of hours are all to be given consideration. Rubber heels mediate happily between the nervous system and the flinty substitutes for the yielding surface of good old mother earth over which our ancestors trod with springy step.

Considerable attention might well be given to method of attack upon pieces of work. The man who is barely under way at ten o'clock in the forenoon is more likely to accomplish a large amount of work than one who wakes early and eats breakfast with agitation. The day can be spoiled by a too early and too intense start in the morning. The time spent in leisurely approach is far from wasted. The mind can be best utilized by charging one's thoughts with a purpose and then allowing the inner resources to crystallize toward achievement. Once the purpose is in mind, subject matter will seem almost to collect itself. Items will drift into consciousness and cement themselves to the main theme. By charging the mind with the general topic, a sort of law of gravitation operates for preparation. Material that would not be noticed if the mind were not charged with the topic will be picked up casually.

Premature effort and worried diligence have little constructive value. Many of the most critical exertions rely upon habit for effective performance. It is a well-known fact that habitual acts are performed most successfully when there is a minimum of attention given to them. Hence it is that insouciance wins victories denied to the Marthas who take too much thought. The speaker probably gives more heed to the introduction of his speech than to succeeding parts, and there is no part that the audience usually would more willingly dispense with. One writes his opening paragraphs with rigid care and is often not unwisely advised to throw away the first pages. Assuming a class of individuals whose affairs tend to exceed possibility of performance, one feels that a closer scrutiny of energy-using methods is highly warranted.

Reinforcement of energy is no less a matter of concern than is the avoidance of positively spendthrift practices. One man finds that he needs to take a "snooze" after the midday meal for a successful day. Another, a university president, goes to bed a short time before appearing on the public platform. One widely known forensic performer does not, for a half day before his public addresses, take part in conversation or allow people to see him. Thus he saves up power for the special occasion.

The individual's energy is not a fixed amount like

the water in a dam. The quantity of energy appears to be governed by various factors, and it is not possible by resting three hundred sixty-five days to have three hundred sixty-five times the normal amount of energy at the expiration of that period. Nevertheless there is unquestionably a "pool" formation for energy over brief periods. Ordinarily, rather brief periods of recuperation suffice to restore the energies, though in cases of extreme fatigue and exhaustion months may be insufficient.

An interesting phase of the subject of energy utilization is that illustrated in "blowing off steam." The angry person who vents his feelings soon subsides to equilibrium and forgets his troubles. Similarly with the man with a big idea who talks himself out on the subject. Refraining from much vocalization the individual would possibly compile a treatise or write a novel or develop an invention or launch a business enterprise. But by oozing interest and wasting the dynamic forces of motive by dissertations in the smoking room, John Doe remains John Doe in a state of exploded incentive. The surest way to lose interest in a new idea of one's own and to check the cerebral irritation that might issue in creation is to give the thought premature exploitation and too much sunlight. Indeed there is such a thing as conversing a subject into too great lucidity and hardening its fiber into the commonplace. The greatest and most inspiring works of literature contain an element of illusion and error. A degree of foggy-mindedness is as necessary to creative genius as dampness is to mushrooms. One reads H. G. Wells and wonders if his immensely suggestive and entertaining production might not have been frozen to the root by rigorous criticism and scrutiny.

The fatal tendency to talk off ideas has oftentimes been counteracted by personal circumstances which the world calls unfortunate. Many great achievements in the intellectual sphere have come from men and women who lacked normal expression. Sickness, deformity, timidity, unsocial disposition, imprisonment—all these interfere with the usual run of experiences and contacts and force the mind to develop unwonted ways of expression. Darwin said that if illness had not kept him out of society he would not have made his scientific researches. The person who has reached that goal of misguided endeavor, perfect correspondence with environment, empties as fast as he fills. The world would be infinitely poorer if deprived of the brain product of men who have been rubbed sore and had no one at hand to tell it to.[1] In the strategy of civilization much depends upon what objectives enlist the mental energies, for serious loss is possible through irrelevant activities. The Middle Ages witnessed a vigorous exercise of mind. The universities were seats of learning, and scholars were diligent and jealous of repute. There were prodigies of scholarly zeal. But with all the fidelity and devotion of capable mind the intellectual output was negligible. The science of the period was insignificant and the literary output was largely the rubbish of scholasticism. The Middle Ages were the blind alley of human thought.

It is not enough that there be intellectual effort; it is important how that effort is organized and to what ends. The types of problems, the issues developed and stated, the objectives of investigations—these count for more than sheer mental ability.

The possession of fine powers of intelligence is no assurance of their profitable use. Individuals highly promising in youth may defeat the hopes of those interested in their success, because of failure to choose profitable aims and to direct energies

[1] A valuable exposition of this thought is found in an article by Wesley Raymond Wells, "Intellectual Value of Physical and Social Maladjustment," *School and Society*, November 12, 1921.

aright. The character of one's ambitions, his interests, his perseverance, his assessment of values, are of more critical significance than mental endowment of itself alone. Often the person of mediocre parts makes the greatest contribution to professional or business development, because he judges well what ends to pursue and what to avoid. Concentration is necessary, joined with suitable objective. A young man may prepare for the law in a night school in the time taken by another of equal mental agility to learn to play a surpassing game of billiards.

Spendthrift use of mental resources, the waste of irrelevance, the taking of false trails, the exaggeration of the insignificant, the searching for gold in the air instead of in the ground, find ample illustration in the lives of men and of communities: hypertrophied and frantic interest in sports and games, wordy, insincere battles for conquest rather than for truth, a mythlike sex romanticism, easeful and cajoling forms of religious languor, the perennial crops of over-advertised fads and salvations that serve to becloud issues, the obsession of money-making, the glut of current information, the treadmill of social conventionality. the corruption of thought to details.

Probably enough mental energy has been consumed in reading detective stories to have served to sift all theories of taxation, marshal all its facts and provide a perfection of theory and practice in this field. Baseball energy, commercially evoked to extravagant proportions, is perhaps equivalent to that required for overcoming illiteracy in a backward country. Invention would know no end if the surplus imagination of sex could be released to science. Civilization would be centuries ahead if insoluble or factitious theological questions had not engaged men's minds for so long and drained the faculties. Imagine the constructive power of a Jonathan Edwards transferred from terroristic speculation to the campaign to humanize or abolish child labor.

Social welfare rests back upon the mental energies and traits of the individual members of society. The functioning of mind is the crucial fact in social organization. Whether higher forms of social integration are possible or not is to be decided by how the individual's mind functions socially in its various aspects of instinctive tendency, habit, attention, memory, observation, conception, reasoning, and motivation. Social disintegration always impends, and no former civilization has escaped the factors of disorganization and lapse, which many have assumed are implicit in individual psychology. Destruction of civilization and even destruction of mankind through wars, the recrudescence of slavery, and a fatal fatigue of constructive effort and of invention and altruistic zeal are a continuing menace. There are not wanting those who hold that the peculiar attributes of human mind and consciousness—so different from animal intelligence and apparently so at odds with the intelligence of nature—originated in a cosmic chance—the supreme blunder of the universe, a blunder that would be canceled by social devolution. The renouncing of the intellectual life, the exaltation of habit, concessions to reflexes and instincts, and the abandonment of painfully sustained strivings would, from this point of view, be quite as natural as continuing the battle.

If mental resources are a worked-out mine, then of course the stage is set for the modern nations to follow in decline the nations that have heretofore risen only to collapse. But if our mental assets are capable of vastly richer development and more skillful employment to social ends, the obvious program is that of utilizing in the best ways our undeveloped resources. It is a fair statement that we know as yet little of the possibilities of mankind. Only the crudest methods have been employed for the conservation and the beneficial exploitation of human faculties. The most interesting of projects is that of redirecting and more fully developing the forces of consciousness. Here is the master undertaking of all the ages. Sociology and psychology are new sciences—scarcely more than new interests. The emphasis of the last two centuries has been on solving problems centering in natural science and in industrial production. The social problem is yet to be attacked with like plentitude of energy and idealism. Though our mental assets show natural and habitual limitations, there is promise that the individual is capable of acquiring an adequate social mind, a mind enlarged and rectified as contrasted with mind to-day.

The large problem of society is to provide joyous outlet for inherited tendencies and constructively to redirect such expressions of instinct as are not in harmony with rational program. Untutored human instinct may lead to as disastrous reactions under the circumstances of newly invented civilization as are witnessed in the case of the moth seeking the open flame through its instinctive tropism to light. Increasingly man finds need of revising his instinctive tendencies in the interest of safety, progress, and social stability. The guidance afforded by impromptu consciousness is and has always been costly and deficient.

In earlier and more rudimentary stages of human society, the largeness of the jurisdiction of instincts pure and simple and the narrow and timid reliance upon higher intelligence, were associated with a multitude of evils and oppressions. The individual who does not bring his impulses under analysis, and in many instances flout his instinctive promptings, is incapable of the greatest usefulness to society, and is doomed to a personal inferiority in terms of worldly success and achievements resting upon sustained attention and self-restraint. Just in proportion to the conscious regulation of natural tendency and the correlative exaltation of the higher powers of adaptation, do individuals and society achieve prosperity. The criminal class is a class with whom instinct prevails; savages live by instinct. Masses of people, in recent centuries of partial civilization, exemplify exuberant activity of the tendencies that formed the mind of prehistoric man. Here and there throughout the ages have appeared the man, the group, the school who, by sunlit lives, have shown the race the kindliness and creativeness possible when the expressions of instinct have been refined. The future belongs to the great natural motivations of instinct illuminated by logical analysis, developed attention, self-restraint, verified knowledge, and disciplined imagination.

INDEX

(1)